Life's Not Over, It Just Looks Different

by Christopher Warner

First printed: 2016

ISBN 978-1-365-45152-2

TO BOB & DARLING,

IT'S NOT WHAT YOU SEE
IT'S HOW YOU LOOK AT IT.

— CW

Life's Not Over, It Just Looks Different

For Cindy

THAT FIRST MORNING

When I opened my eyes the morning of October 21, 2005, I could only make out light and shadows. I looked around the room. Everything was in shades of grey and not clearly defined.

I must still be groggy from the surgery, I thought to myself. I couldn't really tell if I was fully awake or not, but I thought I must be only half awake, because I couldn't focus on anything.

A shadowy figure appeared in the doorway of my hospital room.

"Hi." It was Cindy, my wife of nine years.

"Hi."

"The nurses told me you're not eating your lunch," she said. "Are you *not* hungry?"

"My lunch?" I reached out to the tray table in front of me, feeling around and accidentally touching the breaded piece of meat that was to be my meal that afternoon.

"Aren't you going to use your utensils?" Cindy asked.

"Oh yeah, good idea." I felt around for my fork and started to eat. The breaded cutlet didn't taste like much and the vegetables had been boiled too long — typical hospital food. Cindy and I continued talking between bites. I looked up from my food to say something else to her.

"Why are you still talking to me over there?" she asked, in a slightly annoyed tone. She had moved to the other side of the bed.

"Oh, I didn't realize you had moved."

"How many fingers am I holding up?" Cindy asked, copying a quick test she had seen the doctors do with me.

"I can't see your fingers, but I think I see your hand."

"Follow my hand with your eyes."

She moved her hand up, to the left and then to the right.

That's when we discovered I had a problem.

"I'll be back in a minute."

She touched my feet as she walked past the end of the bed and quickly out the door to the brightly-lit hallway.

Alone again in the hospital room, I was trying to make sense of what just happened. *Why wasn't I able to see her fingers?*

This wasn't my first shunt surgery. In the past two days there had been two operations because the first one hadn't worked; bringing the total number of shunt revisions to 13 over my lifetime.

I thought back to the shunt revision in 2001. That surgery went smoothly. In fact, I woke up so abruptly in the recovery room, I startled the nurse. I felt well enough following that operation to return to work two days after being released from the hospital. This time though, four years later, something was different, but neither of us understood yet what it was.

At the nurses' station, a short distance down the hall from my hospital room, Cindy tried to get the attention of a nurse to tell her about her concern. A group of nurses were huddled together talking behind the desk.

"Excuse me," Cindy said.

The nurses stayed in their huddle.

"Excuse me." Cindy persisted until one of them came over to her.

"My husband can't see."

The nurse just looked back at her, unfazed by Cindy's statement.

"You don't get it. My husband can't see. My husband came to this hospital able to see."

Life's Not Over, It Just Looks Different

at's when the hospital learned I had a problem.

Early years

was born with a condition called hydrocephalus — water on the brain. My body produces a higher than normal amount of cerebrospinal fluid (CSF), and the build-up of extra fluid puts tremendous pressure on the brain because it has nowhere to drain off and the body cannot absorb it fast enough.

Hydrocephalus is incurable but treatable. The most common treatment for the condition is surgery to implant a shunt to drain off the fluid. The shunt consists of a unidirectional valve that sits on the skull under the skin and is connected to two catheters. The proximal catheter runs from the valve, through a small burr hole in the skull to the cerebral ventricles of the brain. The distal catheter runs from the valve down the right side of my body. The fluid from the ventricles of the brain flows freely through the catheters to another part of the body where the fluid can be better absorbed, thus relieving the pressure on the brain.

My first shunt was implanted when I was three months old. At that time, back in the early 1970s, the surgery was fairly new and not being performed at hospitals in all cities — and certainly not in the hospital of my small hometown of Atikokan, Ontario. I was flown to Winnipeg,

Manitoba, and taken to Winnipeg Children's Hospital — the closest hospital doing the procedure at that time.

The original shunt was placed on the right side of my head just above my ear. The catheter ran down my neck on the right side and across my body to drain into my heart — a ventriculoatrial (VA) shunt. Having the shunt drain into my heart was the doctor's location of choice until 1979.

Despite almost annual surgeries to adjust the shunt, I had a fairly normal childhood — regular public schools, pretty good grades, and I didn't look any different from my classmates and friends. Up to about the age of nine, classmates were all made aware of my condition. Some made fun of me, but most seemed fascinated that I had what they called a "tube and a button" inside my body that they couldn't see.

The only thing missing from my childhood was contact sports. There was always a risk of damage to the shunt if I got hit in the head or anywhere along the path of the catheter, so no hockey or football, and in gym class I had to wear a hockey helmet to protect my head from injury, even for basketball.

The yearly trips to Winnipeg for shunt revisions continued throughout most of the 1970s. In 1979, I went to a hospital in Thunder Bay, Ontario, a city closer to my hometown, where the surgery was now being done. During that revision, the surgeon decided to change the distal catheter location so it would no longer drain into my heart.

Life's Not Over, It Just Looks Different

Instead, he moved it to my abdomen —a ventriculoperitoneal (VP) shunt. It wasn't fed into any particular organ, but allowed to float somewhat freely in the peritoneal cavity.

Despite my parents' best efforts to keep me from getting involved in any activities that would damage the shunt, kids are kids and sometimes kids get hurt — even me. Being an active young boy, I found ways to get hurt where nobody expected it to happen — like slipping and falling at a bowling alley. The toboggan accident was a little scarier.

It was just after Christmas 1979, and our small town was having a sliding party. Hundreds of people were there, sliding down the hill on toboggans or inner tubes and enjoying the day. The main event that night was a huge bonfire, fuelled by the discarded Christmas trees, that lit up the night sky, bathing the hill and the townspeople in its glow.

My aunt and uncle took me to the party that day. The three of us spent hours at the hill, sliding down the bumpy, snow packed surface and then climbing back to the top to do it all over again.

We were going to call it a day, but I wanted to get in one more slide before we left. I fell off the toboggan part way down the hill and, according to my aunt, before I could get out of the way, a large inner tube with nine people on it came down and hit me in the head. Helpless to stop it from happening, my aunt and uncle ran over from where they were standing at the bottom of the hill. I'm told the ambulance came right away and took me to the hospital, my aunt riding by my side. Fearing the shunt had been affected by the impact, I was rushed by ambulance to Thunder Bay to have it checked.

The shunt was revised as a result of the accident, but when I didn't recover quickly afterward, the doctor investigated and found that the shunt was not functioning, so I was taken back in for a second revision. During the second surgery, the neurosurgeon discovered another complication: the valve had fused to my brain and couldn't be removed without causing more damage. He left it in place and installed a new valve at a different spot, five centimetres above the old valve location, near the top of my head. This time, the neurosurgeon also put in an extended length of distal catheter for me to *grow into* as he put it and, with any luck, I wouldn't have to return to the hospital annually for a revision. His plan worked much better than expected. I didn't have to go for another revision until 2001 — 21 years later.

MY HEAD HURTS

I woke up with an awful headache one Friday morning in July 2001 and couldn't stand up for very long without feeling nauseated. I called in sick to work that day, thinking it was a sinus headache or flu. I took a sinus pill and tried to sleep it off. I loved my job in the broadcast operations department at Global TV, so it wasn't like me to miss a day of work, especially for a cold or a headache, but on that day, I wasn't going anywhere. The headache didn't go away, and when Cindy came home that evening, she was very concerned and took me to the hospital.

Cindy and I had moved to Toronto only 18 months earlier. It was a much larger broadcast market, and we wanted to take the next step in our broadcast careers as videotape operators for Global TV. Being fairly new to the city, we didn't know if there was a specific hospital for shunt care, so we went to the nearest hospital in north Toronto. It had been so long since I'd had any problem with the shunt that finding out which hospital to go to hadn't been high on my list of priorities when we made the move from Regina.

The emergency room doctor at North York Hospital advised us to go immediately to Sunnybrook (a large trauma hospital) because his hospital wasn't able to deal with neurological cases. I give that doctor a lot of credit for listening to me and not wasting any time looking for some other problem.

In the emergency department at Sunnybrook, when I told them about my shunt, it felt like everyone I spoke to wanted to challenge me. I felt like nearly every resident or nurse I spoke with didn't believe me when I told them I thought I might be having a shunt problem. Their reaction was frustrating to say the least. By the time we were at the hospital, I had pretty much ruled out any idea that this was a typical headache. This was something more, something I hadn't felt in a long time. My head really hurt and the nausea was unusual for me, too. I rarely feel sick to my stomach. I have a pretty good understanding of my body, and I knew something was really wrong. What I needed now was for someone to listen to me!

One of the residents told us she wanted to do a nuclear medicine test, but the department was closed for the weekend. She advised us to go home and someone would be in touch with us on Monday to make the appointment. The fact that she wanted to do the nuclear medicine test suggested that she believed what I was telling her, but then she went on to say that they suspected I had nothing more than a migraine headache. Perhaps she didn't believe me, after all. I was given some prescription pain killers and sent home.

That was on Saturday. I stayed in bed all day Sunday, coping the best I could with the pain, because the pills were only giving me short-term relief.

Monday came and went with no phone call. Cindy and I went back to emergency on Tuesday morning. I told the triage nurse what had taken place on Saturday and about the phone call that never happened. She took my personal information and asked us to sit in the waiting area for my name to be called.

So, we waited. When they finally called my name, I walked slowly behind the nurse as she escorted me to a bed. I began feeling very nauseated and asked to lie down.

"Just a moment," the nurse said.

"No. *Now* — please!" I leaned onto the nearest empty bed and started vomiting.

Six hours later, after a million questions from a number of nurses and residents, a doctor came up and checked my shunt. He pressed it and waited a few seconds.

"You're right," he said. "It's not working. You're going in for surgery as soon as we can get you in."

I was admitted to hospital and placed in the Neuro Intensive Care Unit (NICU) to await surgery. They didn't have an open operating room, but wanted me ready to go in at any time, so I couldn't have anything to eat.

Again, I waited. It was 9:30 p.m. before the nurse finally told me there would be no surgery that day. By that time, I was really hungry. I had been hooked up to an IV pole, and they had given me something to settle my stomach, so I was no longer feeling the nausea from earlier in the day. I knew I couldn't eat before the surgery, but now that there would be no operation that day, getting something to eat was my sole focus. The nurse apologized because they didn't have a food tray for me at that late hour and the kitchen was closed. Closed? Really? One of the biggest hospitals in the city and they don't even have a sandwich to feed a patient in the middle of the night? I was shocked. The nurse called Cindy and asked her to bring me something to eat.

"What do you think she'll bring you at this hour?" the nurse said as she checked the blood pressure read out.

"She'll likely bring in the half cantaloupe we have in the fridge and a bottle of Coke," I said. The nurse looked at me, her eyes wide.

"You don't think she'll stop at McDonald's?" she asked.

"No, she'll probably bring me the cantaloupe."

I was right. My dinner that night consisted of a half cantaloupe, a bottle of Coke and a bag of potato chips.

There would be no surgery on Wednesday, either, and by that time I was feeling a mix of frustration, impatience and anxiety. When the hospital staff came to tell me there'd be no operation that day, I couldn't help myself. I broke down in tears and buried my face in a pillow, partly from the frustration and the stress of waiting so long for surgery, but the pillow was to cover the embarrassment of bawling my

Life's Not Over, It Just Looks Different

eyes out in front of a group of medical residents. A nurse came by a short time later.

"We called your wife and asked her to come in to help settle you down," she said.

That wasn't a good thing to do — it just upset Cindy, too. When she arrived at the hospital, we held each other tight as we both sobbed our hearts out. After a few minutes, we both calmed down as we sat beside each other on the side of the bed, snuggled up close together, each of us feeling better knowing our best friend was by our side.

My breakdown must've had some effect on the staff, because they came back a short time later to tell me I'd be in for surgery the next afternoon.

Through all of this, Cindy was beside herself. Her husband of five years was in hospital about to go in for brain surgery that she was pretty sure was serious, and the medical staff wasn't fixing it. To make matters worse, we had only been in Toronto for a while so she had no family nearby and didn't know anyone outside of work. By the time I finally went in for surgery two days after being admitted, she was in bad shape. She still had to go to work, which she said provided a bit of distraction, but she wasn't sleeping properly, was seriously stressed about me being in the hospital for brain surgery, and had no one at home to help occupy her time. Luckily, a very sweet and caring co-worker of ours who lived across the road from us had heard about me being in the hospital and invited Cindy to stay with her for a few days so she didn't have to be alone.

I wasn't nervous about the surgery until I was on my way to the operating room on Thursday afternoon. This was my first time going in for surgery as an adult, so to be honest, I didn't really know what to expect. The only thing I could remember from my surgeries as a kid was the black anaesthesia mask being placed over my mouth and nose and the horrible smell of the gas they used to put me to sleep. I did my best to hide my uneasiness as I sat on the bed. It was parked in the hallway, waiting to be wheeled in, and I chatted with one of the staff about some of our favourite sports heroes. He interrupted our conversation when he noticed I had signed the consent form, but it didn't say what the operation was going to be.

"That's a dangerous thing to do when the form hasn't been signed by the doctor," he said.

I chuckled and told him that if I came out of the room with a hysterectomy, they were all going to be in trouble!

The operation took about two hours.

As I was being wheeled out of the recovery room and back to the ward, I saw Cindy talking to a friend on a payphone in the hallway. She hung up immediately and came to join me on my way to my room.

Life's Not Over, It Just Looks Different

I was told if everything worked out well I'd be discharged on Saturday morning, but when Saturday arrived, there were no doctors with the authority to sign me out. I waited and waited, pestering the nurse looking after me to take the IV out of my hand.

"I can't do that yet," she said.

"But I'm going home today," I protested. "I don't need it anymore. I feel great."

"But if I take it out and then something happens, I don't want to have to put it back in," she said, not willing to give in.

I pleaded with her every time she came by my room until she finally gave in and removed it.

I went home Saturday afternoon and called work to tell them I was home; alive and well. I wanted to return to work on Monday, but my manager told me to take as long as I needed to recover. I went back Tuesday.

Upon my return to work that morning, a few of my co-workers had questions about what had happened and how I was feeling. It was obvious that something was different, because I was wearing a baseball cap at work, something I didn't normally do. The cap was to cover the fact that my head was completely shaved and to conceal the rather large bandages covering my iodine-stained scalp and the 17 staples holding the skin together on either side of the incision the doctor had made.

This was the first time in a long time I was getting questions about the shunt from those around me. I didn't mind the questions, although the more often I was asked, the shorter the story got. A few people asked if they could see the staples on my head. I was a little hesitant at first, because I didn't want to gross them out. I warned anyone who asked that it was not a pretty sight and on that warning some decided they didn't want to see what was under the hat. For those who were really curious, I lifted the hat off my head, exposing the large white gauze bandage and then gently peeled back some of the tape that held it in place so they could see the staples. Their curiosity satisfied, most of them just walked away saying they were glad I was okay.

After the shunt revision, I began doing internet research on hydrocephalus. Although I'd been living with the condition for 30 years, there were gaps in my knowledge, and getting information from doctors wasn't easy. The stories and reports I read online during my research told of people who grew up with any number of learning or physical disabilities. Like any disease or condition, people experience it in different ways; some go through life with very few problems, while others face daily challenges. Other people's experiences with hydrocephalus made me realize I was pretty lucky, despite having to have brain surgery every now and then.

Life's Not Over, It Just Looks Different

Cindy became a little more watchful of my health after that surgery. Any time I told her I had a headache, she would ask if it was one of *those* headaches — her way of asking if she should be taking me to the hospital. I would either tell her no, I'm pretty sure it's nothing more than a normal headache, or I'd tell her I was going to take a pain pill and keep her posted. Very often, that was the right course of action, because I didn't want to run to the hospital for every headache. I didn't want to cry wolf, and the wait time in the hospital emergency was just too long. I didn't want to spend six hours or more in the hospital for something that could be treated with a pain pill and a good night's sleep.

With the surgery behind us, life picked up pretty much where it had been before. I resumed all of my normal activities, working, going to races and go-kart racing. It felt good to get back to the local tracks where I watched my friends race on Friday and Saturday nights. I waited a week or two longer, until I was sure my scalp was fully healed, before slipping on my own helmet and rejoining the other competitors at the go-kart track where I competed most Monday nights.

EARLY WARNING

The first hint of trouble with the shunt was in late December 2003. I woke up one morning with a sharp pain in my lower right abdomen. It was an intense localized pain that made it hurt even to breathe. If I even sneezed or took a sudden deep breath, I would get a jolt of pain in my right side so painful, it made me fear the next one.

I was scheduled to work at 4 p.m. that afternoon, and probably should have called in sick, but instead I put on my coat and shoes and headed out the door to begin the walk to work. It normally took about 10 minutes to walk the three blocks, but I left extra early that day. I walked slowly down the street, standing up as straight as possible, because slouching seemed to hurt more.

Sitting in front of the master control console didn't stop the pain from making its presence known. Throughout the first half of my shift, I tried to control my breathing, taking slow, steady breaths, but the pain flared up anyway.

Each time it did, I gasped, which made me take a deep breath, which hurt even more. I gritted my teeth, put my right hand on my abdomen and tried to regulate the pace of my breathing until the pain subsided. *Maybe I should go to the hospital to get this checked out*, I thought. But my next thought would be about waiting for hours at the hospital, and I really didn't want to go there.

Five hours into that night shift, I decided to call Ontario's telephone health service. I thought that at least this way, if they said I should go to the hospital, it was less likely to turn out to be nothing.

After a number of questions, the nurse on the phone said, "You should go to the hospital right away." I asked her what she thought it was, but she said she couldn't tell me and repeated her recommendation to go to the hospital right away. I told her I was at work and wouldn't be able to leave on such short notice, because there was no one there to cover my shift. She didn't like that answer.

Ultimately, I told her I'd go to the hospital right after my shift was over, and we ended the call. I figured if I had been putting up with it for this long I could wait three more hours. The pain didn't get any better, but it didn't get any worse, either, as I waited for my shift to end. And it wasn't really interfering with my work, unless I needed to get up out of the chair to find a videotape or go to the washroom. If I had to get out of the chair, I did it very slowly and gently, raising myself up from being bent over at the waist into a fully upright position. It didn't take that long to do it, but if I forgot and tried to stand up too quickly, it really hurt — so I didn't rush.

When I finished my shift at midnight, I went to the hospital and told the emergency nurse about my conversation with the nurse on the phone. She went through her normal triage questions and then asked me to wait for the doctor. A few minutes later, I was shown to a small cubicle where I sat on the bed and waited. I could hear her update the doctor when she arrived.

"I think it may be his appendix."

"No, it's not my appendix," I countered as they came close.

"Sir, there's a scar on your lower abdomen — you haven't had your appendix removed?"

"No," I said. "That scar is from a previous shunt operation."

"It looks like an appendix scar to me," the doctor said.

"Unless it was removed as a preventative measure in a previous shunt surgery, I still have my appendix."

"If you were unconscious and I saw that scar, I would think it was from an appendix operation."

"Then it's a good thing I'm not unconscious," I said with a cheeky tone and a grin.

After a couple of hours of waiting, I was sent for a CT scan of my abdomen. Still lying on the bed in emergency, a porter wheeled me through the hospital to the diagnostic imaging department, and into the room where they would do the CT scan. With the help of the porter and the radiology technician, I slid gently from the hospital bed onto the table for the test.

They performed the regular CT scan and then a rectal contrast test. I'd never had one before and I hope never to experience it again. The test is an enhanced CT scan. A rigid tube is inserted in the rectum and held in place by expanding a balloon, which keeps the tube in place. A bag of water is then fed through the tube, filling the colon until the bag is empty, which makes the colon easier to see. As my body filled with water, my muscles had the sudden urge to try and push the tube out. The pain was horrible! I began to twitch and twist my body around, but wasn't able to get very far, because the balloon was holding the tube firmly in place. I moaned and groaned, gasping each time the pain increased.

"Just relax," the technician said. "Try to relax."

It wasn't easy, but I took a few deep breaths, and soon the pain subsided enough that I was able to relax for the rest of the test.

The doctor reviewed the CT, but found nothing conclusive. The emergency doctor gave me some pain killers and sent me home — Percocet, a potentially addictive pain killer. It relieved my abdominal pain, but made me feel light headed. I had other sensations that I'd never experienced before and can't really explain, except to say I felt weird. I've never taken any recreational drugs, but if that's what being high felt like, I didn't like it. Over the next three days, I tried my best to avoid taking the medication until the pain was unbearable. Ultimately, it went away completely.

As a result of the inconclusive finding from the tests at the emergency department, I was referred to a general surgeon who looked over the CT results. He thought the pain I had experienced was caused by the lower end of the shunt catheter and referred me to the neurosurgeon I had seen in 2001 for further investigation. The neurosurgeon was not convinced the shunt was causing the problem.

In the end, he told me he saw no good reason to go in and perform what he deemed to be an unnecessary shunt revision. There would be many more shunt revisions in my future and, because there is always a risk of complications or infection, he didn't want to do an operation he didn't feel was warranted.

A few months later, I had another episode of the abdominal pain, and the situation described above repeated itself. This time though, when the CT scan came back with no clear answer, the surgeon requested an ultrasound on my abdomen, but it too showed nothing that compelled the neurosurgeon to act.

This pain flared up six more times over the next 18 months. Each time a CT scan was done, I saw the general surgeon, followed by the neurosurgeon. Finally, one of the CT scans showed a build-up of fluid at the base of the distal catheter near my liver. The neurosurgeon said he finally saw evidence the shunt might be the culprit. If it flared up again, he'd go in and revise the lower end of the shunt. He also talked about moving it to a new location in the pleural cavity near the right lung, so the catheter could not irritate organs in my abdomen.

Life's Not Over, It Just Looks Different

I had another flare up in September 2005. The neurosurgeon scheduled surgery for late October to revise and move the lower end of the shunt. After all, this catheter had been in my body for 25 years. It was probably tired.

A CHANGE IN PLANS

In October 2005, I was working as a master control supervisor for Global TV in Toronto. Broadcasting had been my dream career from the time I was 12 years old and I worked hard to make that happen. When I saw the master control room and the high level of responsibility placed on the people who worked there, I knew it was the role I wanted. I got a taste of working in master control during the early '90s on a part-time basis and then moved to Regina to take a full-time spot in master control before going to Toronto to move my career another step forward. I have always believed it's better to go after the role I want, rather than waiting for the opportunity to come to me.

A few weeks after the neurosurgeon decided he would revise the shunt, I was back in his office for a pre-operative appointment, ten days before the scheduled surgery. He asked how I was feeling. I told him I had a headache, but I wasn't sure if it was anything serious at the time.

Two days after seeing the doctor, I was scheduled to work the midnight shift in a new master control room I had been training in for weeks. The headache I had mentioned to the doctor was still with me. I thought it might be a sinus problem. I didn't feel a cold coming on, but I sometimes experience nasty headaches from sinus colds, so that was my first thought. I'm not a fan of going to the hospital and I feel foolish if it turns out to be nothing, which had happened in the past, so I preferred to rule out things like sinus headaches before assuming it was a shunt problem.

Life's Not Over, It Just Looks Different

I went to work as scheduled at midnight and worked the whole shift. There were two of us working in the new master control environment that night and, according to my co-worker, I didn't look very good by the end of it. I'm told I did my work without saying much, but he hadn't thought much of it because it was midnight shift and it's not uncommon to be tired, although being quiet is a little out of character for me. About an hour before my shift ended, I walked down the hall from master control to one of the videotape rooms to see Cindy, who was also working the midnight shift that night.

"Hi. How's it going?" she asked.

"My head really hurts and I'm having trouble concentrating," I said. "You're going to have to drive home."

"Okay," was all she said.

At home, I tried to sleep but kept thrashing around in pain and moaning, according to Cindy, which kept her awake. After a couple of hours, she decided enough was enough. I think the experience of 2001 not only showed her what to expect but also what to look out for and when it was more than just a headache. She woke me up and told me to cancel a few appointments I had for the next two days. One of the appointments I cancelled that day was a recording session for the next episodes of my show on VoicePrint, a reading service for the vision impaired where I volunteered on a weekly basis. I can only hope it and the other phone conversations I had that morning were coherent, because I have no recollection of them at all.

The trip to Sunnybrook hospital from our place passed through an upscale older neighbourhood in north Toronto. Parts of the road are built with paving stones instead of concrete or asphalt, and there are large speed bumps along the way. Cindy drove very slowly through this area to keep from aggravating my pain.

I remember walking into the hospital and talking to the triage nurse. I told her I had surgery booked for the coming week but that I was really hurting now. While we sat in the waiting room, I felt sick to my stomach and went to the washroom, but only got dry heaves.

When I came out of the washroom, Cindy told me the nurse had been calling for me. Just like in 2001, I threw up in the emergency room. One of the doctors told me later that throwing up was actually one of the signs that lets them know a shunt problem is occurring.

I recall very little of the next few days in hospital, so I asked Cindy to be my eyes and ears. Her memory of what happened is as devastating as mine was patchy:

A resident saw Chris right away, surprisingly. Shortly after, the head emergency doctor came by and tested him. When the nurse finally came, Chris was shaking. She gently asked him if he was cold and if he could stop shaking because she needed to put an IV in his arm.

Chris couldn't stop shaking, and so she called in another nurse to put in the IV. I was more worried because Chris was in so much pain.

Hours passed and finally the shunt doctor came by. He introduced himself, took a quick look at Chris's chart and then put it down at the end of the bed to focus on Chris. He felt the back of Chris's head so he could be familiar with the location of the shunt reservoir, but didn't press it. Then he held up one finger in front of Chris and asked him if he could follow it. Chris couldn't look up. The farthest he could look up was straight. This was around 8 p.m.

"Well, Mr. Warner," the doctor began, as he took a step back and folded his arms across his chest, "you definitely can't wait until next week for surgery, but the surgical team has gone for the night and your condition isn't serious enough to justify after-hours emergency surgery."

My heart sank. They wanted to book the surgery for early the next morning and tried to get Chris to sign a form for surgery, "just in case he became worse and needed the surgery sooner," but he was in too much pain and pushed it away. I signed it for him. The doctor came back to tell us that as soon as they had a bed free in NICU they would move him.

Chris was finally looking calmer, almost sleeping, but he was still restless. My instinct told me to ask the doctor to look him over again.

The doctor did acknowledge Chris was resting better, didn't want to wake him up. In the end, I didn't ask.

As soon as the doctor left, a nurse came and moved us to a different location, away from the desk. She asked me if I could stay and watch Chris because they had another patient that needed more constant observation. The room they moved us to was completely enclosed, with walls and a door rather than a sliding curtain. I felt very isolated, brushed aside in favour of the next case. I watched Chris for some time, until I remembered that I had to run home to feed the cats. When I came back, I watched Chris for a while, but then realized I needed to get some sleep, too. The nurse had suggested it to me earlier, telling me not to worry because the monitoring devices he was hooked up to would definitely wake me up if anything was wrong. I took small comfort from that, but I was exhausted. When the nurse came back with a blanket, I fell asleep almost immediately. I kept waking up about every hour or two, though, to check on Chris. Suddenly, around three in the morning they moved us to acute emergency.

It was so noisy, there was no chance of further sleep. Closed off from the rest of the emergency department, this section had ten patients and five staff. But, again, we were shoved into a corner, in a semi-private area and almost ignored. A nurse came in once in a while to check on Chris's vital signs, but, really, how could they tell if he was getting worse or not? They didn't ask any questions about how he was doing until about 2 p.m. It was finally a doctor who asked him how long he had been that way. I said all night and most of the afternoon. As she

Life's Not Over, It Just Looks Different

walked away to the opposite corner, I heard her say, "Warner is to go to NICU, now." Her voice was tight and authoritative. I understood what she meant: they should have moved him sooner.

Part of me wished I had said something to the nursing staff sooner; perhaps they would've called in a doctor to look Chris over. On the other hand, sometimes nurses get angry or annoyed if they feel they're being pestered by family members of a patient, and then they can become even less helpful or communicative.

There was a time when we trusted doctors and nurses to see the signs of a patient needing more care or who was deteriorating. More recently, however, there are so many demands being placed on doctors and nurses that it's falling to loved ones to watch over patients. Where that falls apart is that family members are not medical experts and their judgment can be clouded by worry for the patient. And that's the balancing act that took place. I wanted to ask them to check on Chris more often, but didn't want to risk having them shut me out, ignore me, or even tell me to go home and let them do their job. We'll never know if asking about Chris's condition sooner would've made the staff do anything different, but at least this doctor seemed to be on top of it and was reacting quickly.

I followed as they took him upstairs and casually asked, "Do you know if they are going to do the surgery soon? The doctor told me they were going to do it in the early morning."

"I don't know," she said.

I think she didn't want to let on how bad she thought Chris was and that they should have checked on him earlier in the day, as they had told me they would.

Chris went to NICU and I knew the drill. I had to stay in a waiting room until they were organized. So, I went into the waiting room, and as soon as I sat down they called.

"Chris is going into surgery; do you want to meet him in the hallway?" the nurse asked me.

"Sure. This is what he's been waiting for."

"Can you take off his unnecessary jewellery?" a nurse asked.

We had a hard time taking off his wedding ring. But all of a sudden, Chris himself took it off and gave it to me. I put it on my left index finger and gave him a kiss goodbye.

I went back to the waiting room and sat down and looked at his ring on my finger. Then, I looked at all the other rings on my other hand, my father's pinkie ring and my mother's engagement ring. I felt a sudden urge to run down the hallway after them and give Chris's ring back to him, but all I could manage was to ask how long the surgery was going to be. They said an hour or more. It took six.

Life's Not Over, It Just Looks Different

Around 8:30 p.m. I called on the hospital phone to ask if I could visit Chris. They let me in. He seemed so tired and not as alert as the last time he'd had this surgery in 2001. I made it a very quick hi and goodbye and went home. I'd been there all night, and we both needed sleep.

My only memory from Cindy's visit with me after the surgery was a very short chat about the oxygen tube in my nose. I remember touching the tube and telling her they (the nurses) should be taking it out soon.

The next afternoon when Cindy came to visit me in the hospital, she was concerned that I didn't look very good and went to tell the nurses. I think that's one of the good things that came out of the 2001 surgery. It showed Cindy what it looks like when things go well. I believe that prepared her to start asking questions when things weren't going as smoothly as in the past. They told her they knew I wasn't well and that more tests were planned for me that day. The tests weren't done until late afternoon, but they showed I would need another operation. According to the hospital records, a neurosurgical resident called the surgeon at around 6 p.m. to tell him about the test results, and those same records show the surgeon's response was that I could wait until the morning. Two hours later, I had deteriorated to the point that I could not wait until morning. The surgery needed to happen that night. Meanwhile, Cindy had gone home for some rest and to wait for the doctor's call telling her what they planned to do next. She got a call at 9:30 p.m. telling her I was going in for another operation at one in the morning. They asked her how quickly she could get to the hospital. She called our friend Kelly, and asked for a ride to the hospital.

When they arrived, I was later told, I didn't look good. I was breathing very deeply and snoring. As the two of them stood next to my bed, Cindy says she patted my shoulder to try and wake me.

"Chris," she said softly.

"Chris," she tried again, but told me later that I didn't respond at all.

She turned to a nurse standing nearby.

"Did you give him something to help him sleep? I can't seem to wake him up." The nurse said they hadn't.

They called the doctor in to check on me. According to Cindy, when the doctor came in, he grabbed me by both shoulders and shook me very hard, but I still didn't wake up. Cindy said she was really worried at that point because nobody should have been able to sleep through the shaking the doctor had given me.

Kelly later told me that what she saw next was like a scene out of a movie. The doctor pried open one of my eyes to check it, but there was nothing but white. Talking to her after the surgery, Kelly told me, "You weren't there." The doctor called the OR and my surgery was moved up by two hours; from 1 a.m. to 11 p.m.

Life's Not Over, It Just Looks Different

Hearing Cindy and Kelly's account of what happened that night really startled me. The only time I had ever seen a person who was breathing deeply and snoring loudly the way they described, was when I saw a close family member in the last hours of her life. She had been declared brain dead, but her body didn't know it yet. If that was how I looked on that night in the hospital, then I'm convinced that Cindy saved my life when she told the nurse she couldn't wake me.

The next day we all found out just how well the surgery turned out.

I don't remember if the nurses ever told me the food tray was sitting in front of me the day after the surgery. If they did, I don't recall, so when Cindy arrived and asked me about the food tray, that was the first I knew of it.

It hadn't dawned on me yet that I was having trouble seeing. I think I was tired and a little groggy, so not being able to find the tray in front of me just by looking for it reinforced my feeling of still being half asleep. Feeling around for the food felt like a dream. My eyes were probably closed; I was "sleep eating" so to speak, and really only doing so because Cindy mentioned it and not because I felt hungry. Cindy thought sticking my fingers in the food was odd, too, but it didn't fully register with either of us that something more might be wrong. It wasn't until she tested my eyes the way the surgeons did that either of us knew there was something very wrong. That's when she went to find the nurse.

Cindy's revelation to the nurses that I could not see set off a flurry of activity, beginning with a visit from the neurosurgical resident moments after she broke the news. They took me for an MRI to get a better look at my brain to try and figure out why a man who had come into the hospital fully sighted just two days earlier was now reporting he couldn't see.

My neurosurgeon reviewed the MRI results and came to break the news. He said the pressure from the fluid around my brain had put tremendous pressure on the blood vessels leading to the occipital lobe, the part of the brain that processes sight, and that since the operation had relieved that pressure, my blood would now have a chance to flow again as it should.

"We should know how much of your sight will return in about a year," he said.

"Will I get it all back?" I asked, trying to remain calm but inwardly praying he wouldn't say no!

"I'm not sure. We'll have to wait and see what happens in a year," the doctor replied.

I took a moment to process what he just said. Then, trying to be proactive, I asked, "Is there anything I can take to help it?"

"No. It just needs time to heal and see what happens."

Life's Not Over, It Just Looks Different

I needed time for the news from the doctor to really sink in. Being still in the hospital those first few days after hearing I wasn't going to see well for the next year didn't mean much to me yet, because in the hospital so many things are done for you. Staff bring in your meals, nurses are always available by hitting the call bell next to the bed, and it wasn't like I was going out for a walk anywhere without being escorted by Cindy or a porter taking me for another test. Not having to do much for myself meant I didn't fully grasp what challenges lay ahead of me once I was back out in the world again.

In fact, I recall that most of my initial thoughts were about how I was going to prove the doctor wrong. The movie in my head had me getting my full sight back and not taking the full year to do it. I truly believed I was going to be the guy who beat the odds and had an awesome story to tell about how I spent a year (or less) legally blind and then got it all back.

A few days later, the occupational therapist had a test for me to do. She held a large object in front of me and asked if I could tell her what it was. I couldn't identify it just by looking at it. Not until I was able to feel it with my hands was I able to tell her it was a capital T made of wood.

The next time the therapist came to see me, she held up a letter-sized piece of paper and asked me to identify what letter of the alphabet was on the page. The image on the sheet of paper was the full size of the page and although I could tell there was something there, I couldn't read it. Once she allowed me to trace the image with my finger, I figured out it was the letter E.

Two weeks before the surgery I had celebrated my 34th birthday. After being fully sighted for all that time and having excellent colour vision, I was going to spend the next year waiting to recover both of those things. I hoped the doctor was right. It would only take a year, right?

RECOVERY BEGINS

I was given a pass to leave the hospital the last weekend in October 2005, ten days after the second operation. Cindy picked me up from Sunnybrook on Friday night and drove me home to our condo. I spent the next two days at home figuring out what I could see and how well I was going to be able to function in the apartment. It felt so good to be home. I'd missed our two cats and being able to sit on the couch and relax with Cindy. The weekend was over too quickly. It was really hard to go back to the hospital Sunday afternoon. I had no idea how much longer I was going to be there. I felt good physically, so I hoped it wouldn't be much longer.

The doctor came to see me on Monday morning.

"How did the weekend at home feel?" he asked.

"I think it went well," I said. "I didn't bump into anything and it felt *really good* to be at home and in my own space."

"That's very good to hear," he said. "I think we'll go ahead and release you today then."

That last line was music to my ears!

The nurse came in a short time later.

"The doctor says he's going to release me today!" I told her, not even trying to contain the smile spreading across my face.

"Oh, I haven't heard anything about that yet," she said. She finished checking my vital signs, took the blood pressure cuff off my arm, and said she was going to go check her paperwork. A few minutes later, she was back with a medical staple remover in her hand.

"You're right, the doctor left notes for me to take the staples out of your head so you can go home."

I left the hospital for good on Halloween day with the hope that everything would be okay in a year. Although the doctor never actually told me how much of my sight I would get back, I was looking forward and believed that, although it might not fully return, it would be close enough to let me carry on my life much as I had before. Except now, I'd have a pretty cool story to tell about losing my sight for a year and getting it back.

Cindy had to work at 4 p.m. that first day out of the hospital. She asked if I wanted to go along because many of our co-workers were asking her for updates on my condition and if I went to the station, everyone could see for themselves that I was alive and well. It was great to visit with everyone and it gave me a chance to speak to my bosses in person. They told me to focus on my health and that they'd have a spot for me when I was ready to return to work. That was a reassuring thought. I visited with everyone on shift a little while longer, and then my supervisor offered me a ride home as he was on his way out anyway. Cindy still had most of her shift left to work, so I accepted.

On the ride home, we talked more about how I felt and what the doctor had said about my recovery. We also talked about how reading was going to be tough for me, at least for the next year. He told me his mother-in-law had a CCTV, a device used by vision impaired people for reading printed materials. He said he was pretty sure she was no longer using it and that he'd get it from her the next time he was at her place.

Once at home, I felt it was time to start letting our relatives know what had happened over the previous week and a half. I had sent most of my aunts and uncles an email telling them about the planned surgery and wanted to catch them up on the sequence of events. Over the next few days, I called relatives all over Western Canada, some of whom I hadn't spoken to in months. It was great to catch up.

As I phoned each person, I was pleased that most did not get upset. Even my mother, who is normally very emotional, was quite calm about the news.

"It doesn't matter. I still have you," she said.

Don't get me wrong, I wasn't looking for anyone to cry for me. I wasn't crying about it and I didn't want anyone else crying, either. It happened and it was a challenge that needed to be faced. Crying was not going to make it heal any faster so, I didn't spend all my time doing that — at least not on the first day.

Tracking the progress

Seventy-two-point font or larger — that's all I could read during the first few days out of the hospital. I wasn't tracing letters or words with my finger anymore, but there were still times when I would look at a word and have to think about it before it actually sank in. It was Cindy's idea to start typing out what I was experiencing; both as a means of tracking my progress and for something to do. Those notes formed the basis for what you're reading now.

When I first started, I couldn't navigate the computer on my own, so Cindy would open up Microsoft Word on the computer, and I would type my little heart out. Once I finished typing for the day, I saved my work and minimized the program, but didn't close it. It was easier to find whenever I felt the need to type some more.

One of the doctors told us that reading was a good way to stimulate my recovery. Cindy took that information and ran with it. For the next few weeks, she showed me a line of letters in progressively smaller font sizes to test my vision. When I started typing full words I used 48-point font. I would have started at 72, but that would only show me about one word per line, and that just wasn't going to cut it, so I pushed myself to read at 48. It was tough at first. Trying to read smaller font sizes gave me a headache after a few minutes, but like any workout, the more I did it, the easier it got.

Roughly six weeks out of the hospital, I started reading at 36-point font. I could recognize individual letters at smaller sizes, but for reading full words, 36 was all I could manage. Most importantly it was an improvement and it gave me an example that I could use to show people my progress in terms that most computer users could understand. Some people told me they went home to their computer and typed in 36 or 48 just to see it with their own eyes. I carried a sheet of paper with different font sizes on it to give anyone who asked about my progress. Showing it on paper was easier than trying to explain it.

Right out of hospital I had trouble with this (72)

After two weeks out of the hospital I could use this (48)

When I write exams it is usually this (28) or this (24)

The smallest I can read as of January 2007 is this. (12)

But if I want to read more quickly, I need this. (20)

I cannot read this. (10)

After the surgery, colours were mostly shades of grey for the first two months. I first realized I was regaining colour recognition in early

Life's Not Over, It Just Looks Different

January 2006 during a visit to the orthodontist. The office had three chairs; one blue, one red and one yellow. I was able to see the colours of the chairs better than I had on the first visit, three weeks earlier. After the appointment, I told Cindy about my discovery. She was excited about it and took me into a few clothing stores at a nearby mall to test me some more. The primary colours of red, blue and yellow came to me fairly easily. It would be a few more weeks before I could successfully identify secondary colours like orange, purple and green. For the moment, I was defaulting to the primary colours. Sometimes, I would see purple as red, sometimes as blue. Constantly on the lookout for more signs of improvement, Cindy often asked me to identify a colour or handed me something to see if I could read it.

Three weeks into January, I was talking to the psychiatrist about the progress of my sight and gave him some idea of how the world looked through my eyes. The fact that my ability to see small things was seriously impaired was disheartening and took the air out of my good feelings.

There were bad days, too

For the most part I'm a pretty happy guy. Years earlier, I had adopted the philosophy, "I am on this planet for fun." I spent a lot of my time smiling, joking and having a good time. There were times during my recovery, especially early on, where my philosophy was definitely put to the test.

Day two out of the hospital, I came face to face with a nasty case of cabin fever. Cindy had once again gone to work for the evening, leaving me alone in our apartment. I made a few phone calls, listened to some music and did my best to keep myself occupied until Cindy came home. I tried watching television for a while, but fresh out of hospital my view of the magic picture box was cloudy. While I could hear what was being said, I wasn't able to see or enjoy the visual information on the screen.

Around 10 p.m. I was bored out of my tree. The boredom turned to a frustration that built up for the next 45 minutes, until I was in tears. I cried for about 10 or 15 minutes and then decided to walk over to visit Cindy at work.

It wasn't a long walk, only about 12 minutes, and it's a straight line with only one major street to cross. I thought it shouldn't be hard to manage. I put on my shoes and jacket, went down the elevator to the lobby and out the front door. As I walked down the street, I began to realize that my vision, already not very good in the daylight, was even worse in the dark. Every building on the street looked the same as the one beside it. I couldn't make out house numbers or read the street signs. The dim light of the streetlights on that quiet residential street provided enough illumination to show me where the sidewalk was in front of me, but not much more. As I walked, I became less and less confident I would find

Life's Not Over, It Just Looks Different

my way. My normally confident gait was reduced to short, hesitant steps. I was moving my head from side to side, like an animal on the lookout for a predator, but at the same time, trying to keep my wits about me and not have a full-on freak out. Then I thought about the busy intersection up ahead that I would have to cross; I wondered if I would be able to cross safely. I'd only been out of the hospital two days, and the outside world was scarier than I ever thought it could be.

I turned back and headed home. I still had the uneasy feeling of each building looking the same as the one next to it, but I had to get back. I couldn't just stand there and wait for Cindy to come find me and help me get home. I took a big breath and reassured myself that I hadn't gone far and would be able to find where we lived. Although the trip out had felt much further, retracing my steps home took less than five minutes. As I got close, I realized our building is very well lit compared to others around it. It wasn't as hard to find as I had first thought. The tension in my shoulders loosened and I started breathing a little more easily. My walking stride increased once I knew home was right in front of me.

Relieved to be safely back in our apartment, I called Cindy at work. The frustration that made me attempt the walk outside, the combination of fear and nervousness on the short walk and the subsequent feeling of failure to achieve my goal all left my body at once and I broke down in tears as I told her what I had tried to do. Cindy was very sympathetic, glad I was back inside safe and sound, but told me not to try that again, especially at night.

Three weeks later, it happened again, but this time it was inside the building — in the fitness room, to be exact. Music, television and phone calls weren't enough to keep my cabin fever at bay, so I went down to the fitness room to exercise, but it didn't help. I was having a lousy night and that was all there was to it. I didn't even try to go for a walk that time. I was still too unsure of myself. When Cindy called to check in on me, I burst into tears on the phone all over again. Cindy was going to be at work for a few more hours yet, so she couldn't do much other than listen to me blubber, and I was at a loss for a way out of my self-pity. As unfair as it all was to Cindy, she did her best to calm me down over the phone, reminding me that once the mobility worker from the CNIB taught me how to get around, I'd be better equipped to go out on my own. It was small consolation at the time. The visit from the mobility specialist was a few weeks away, but I knew she was right. We talked for a little longer and eventually I calmed down.

With any loss, there is always a grieving process and it must be allowed to happen. Otherwise, it can lead to other physical and mental health issues. The true test is how to move from grief back to life and move forward. That first year, I went from sadness to anger and back again at how my life had been changed by the surgery. Over time, I adjusted to life in low resolution and ultimately learned to appreciate the opportunity I was being given to experience life from a different perspective.

Life's Not Over, It Just Looks Different

CALLING IN THE PROFESSIONALS

Shortly after leaving the hospital, one of the first things I did was book an appointment with a psychiatrist. I had already been working with a doctor who was helping me resolve issues I was having over the loss of my father. When I lost my sight, it was nice not to have to wait for a referral to see him. I believe if I hadn't had access to a psychiatrist in those first few weeks out of the hospital, the adjustment would have been much tougher.

I was scheduled to see him the day I went into the hospital, but I called to cancel the appointment, only telling the receptionist that I wasn't feeling well. When I called for a new appointment, I told her a lot had happened in the past couple of weeks and I had a whole bunch of new material for the doctor. She booked me in the next day.

Cindy had never been to the psychiatrist's office with me, because I was always able to go on my own. Now, though, I was reliant on her to get me there. Even without much sight, I managed to direct her where to go, and when we reached the building, I was able to lead her to his office. Luckily for me, the doctor had a very large sign on his door.

He was shocked when I told him what had happened at the hospital. I didn't shed any tears that day, still trying to put on a brave face and looking at the bright side of things as best I could. Plus, the doctors at Sunnybrook told me I should give it a year to see how much sight I'd get back, so a mere few days out of the hospital, I was filled with hope for a big recovery. Up to this point, I'd only been seeing the psychiatrist about every three to four weeks, but with new circumstances to discuss, and lots of bumps in the road ahead, we increased the visits to every two weeks.

About two weeks after I got out of the hospital, an intake worker from the CNIB called and asked a laundry list of questions to determine my needs. After an hour on the phone, she concluded I would benefit from a home visit by a rehabilitation worker, a mobility specialist, a visit to the low-vision clinic and a technology demonstration.

The rehabilitation specialist was the first to call. Her job was to teach me coping strategies for everyday living, such as how to operate appliances. She told me over the phone before we met that she was vision impaired herself, and when she arrived, I discovered she had less sight than I did. With her guidance, Cindy and I marked buttons on the appliances using raised rubber stickers. I would now be able to find the buttons I needed to do laundry or cook with the stove, oven and microwave. She also provided helpful tips on folding money in different ways so I could tell the bills apart. I could read the bills if I had the opportunity to examine them up close, but it was not something I wanted to do in public if I could avoid it. Canadian paper money is all different colours, but having lost most of my ability to identify colour, using that as a way to recognize the bills was not a good option. To make bill recognition easier, the rehabilitation worker also ordered a bill reader for me from the Bank of Canada, which can tell you, either verbally or by using a sequence of vibrations, the denomination of any bills put into the device.

The next call from the CNIB was the organizer of the technology demonstration. This was an opportunity for me to check out some of the tools available to make reading and writing easier. During our visit to the CNIB's showroom, the demonstrator started out by showing Cindy and me a variety of CCTV units. The machine is very much like the old microfiche viewers that were used for years by libraries, parts departments in car dealerships and medical clinics to store patient records. With the CCTV, the book or other printed material is placed on a platform that is moved around under a lens connected to a monitor to magnify the image. It could be adjusted to zoom in, refocus and even invert the image, so that a white page with black font could be changed to white on black, if that contrast was easier for the person to read.

The CCTV unit my supervisor had given me (his mother-in-law's) was an older model that didn't have some of the features of the units I was shown at the demonstration, but it worked just fine. It was one less device I needed to purchase.

The CNIB tech demonstrator also showed us two different software programs; one that would read the screen to me and another called Zoom Text, which could magnify the screen to whatever size I needed.

I was really leaning toward the Zoom Text software, which I found easier to use. Prior to the demonstration, I had a chance to check it out. Two friends, one of whom had recently been declared legally blind, used it. The only problem was that I would have to pay full price if I wanted to pick it up that day. Cindy and I had just completed the purchase of our condo a few months prior to the surgery, so putting out a lot of money for the software was an expense we decided could wait. Instead, I booked an appointment for a needs assessment with the CNIB so I could qualify for government funding to help cover the cost of the software.

Until then, I chose to type things in larger fonts. If I needed to find something on the Internet, Cindy helped me out.

New found freedom

In late November, I got a call from the mobility specialist at the CNIB. During our phone call, we talked about how much and what I could see. We decided that she should bring me an identification cane, which is about half the size of the typical white cane and not quite as thick. Although an ID cane could be used to help me with stairs and such, its primary use was to let others around me know that I might be in need of assistance. I told her about the walk I had attempted weeks earlier and how it didn't go well. She said going out at night was probably not a good idea, especially on the first try. Memory, she said, would really come into play, and with the sight I did have, I would learn to choose my own landmarks in order to find my way around.

Life's Not Over, It Just Looks Different

Four weeks after my first attempt at a walk outdoors on my own, I decided to try again. I needed to talk with a co-worker I hadn't spoken to since before the surgery. With his help, I had been training in the production control room on my own time for a year before going in for surgery. I wanted to explain to him why I hadn't been there to continue the training I had begun with him.

I was sure his department had not been told of my absence and I imagined he and the others in the control room might be a little curious about why I had disappeared.

The idea to train in production control came to me when I found that master control was becoming too automated for my liking. Automation had slowly been taking over master control for a few years, to the point where I began to feel I was doing more data entry than hands-on work, which was my favourite part about the job. Production control on the other hand, and particularly the role of the technical director, was still a very hands-on position at the time.

Production control is the room connected to the studio that puts shows together. In there, the director calls the shots for the cameras, tells the videotape room when to play the video clips and cues the on-air talent, among other things. The technical director sits next to the director in front of a video mixing board (the switcher) that has a myriad of buttons for them to call up whatever camera, video clip or graphic element the director asks for. To me, it was much like master control, but at an even faster pace, and I loved the hands-on aspect of it.

I spent a lot of hours training in production control, hoping that someday, if the opportunity came along, I would be offered a spot on the production team. When I approached the production manager about training in his department, he said if I wanted to learn on my own time and the three technical directors on his team were willing to train me, he was okay with it. All three of the technical directors who worked on the evening shift rotation said they were willing to work with me, so I was there a lot, sometimes working my regular eight-hour shift in master control and staying for another full eight-hour shift to learn as much as I could from my trainers.

While all three of the technical directors were willing to train me, there were varying degrees of how much they would actually let me touch the switcher. One, in particular, let me get my hands on the equipment as much as I was comfortable with, and just a few weeks prior to going in for surgery, I felt I was really hitting my stride in the role. That's why I felt the need to stop by and visit with him. I wanted him to know I hadn't just fallen off the face of the Earth.

It turned out he had heard about my surgery just two days before I went to visit him. A spot had opened up in production control, and they were going to offer it to me. They'd even approached my supervisor to see if I would be interested. He knew I'd been training in production control and likely would have supported me on making the move. Unfortunately, I couldn't take it, because I was home recovering — lousy timing!

Life's Not Over, It Just Looks Different

My solo walk to Global to talk with my production control trainer actually took place a few days before the mobility specialist visited me for the first time, but I used one of the tips she had given me during our initial phone conversation — calling up my memory of that street. Next door to the Global building was a marketing building for a large Canadian corporation. The building had a sign in front of it, adjacent to the driveway of my workplace. I knew if I could find that sign, I would have my bearings. I set out on my journey, which under normal circumstances was only a 12-minute walk, but I went a little slower to make sure I knew where I was and was focused on what was ahead of me. Cindy was already at work that night. I didn't tell her what I had in mind, because I knew she would worry and try to talk me out of it. I decided I'd tell her by letting her see me when I arrived.

Cindy wasn't the only one concerned. There were many people in my life asking me not to take any walks on my own, at least not until the mobility worker had been to see me, but I felt I had to do it to test myself. Like the last time, the decision to go for a walk came to me in the evening when it was dark outside. Not the ideal walking conditions at such an early point in my recovery, but unlike the previous attempt, this time I felt more confident and I was sure I could find the landmarks I needed along the way to guide me. I laced up my shoes, put on my hat and a light jacket before leaving the condo. I went down the elevator, through the lobby of our building and out the front door. Although every building still looked like all the others, this time I relied much more on my memory for my sense of direction. I walked up the small incline of our street toward my destination, but this time my fear was replaced by a sense of determination. As I made my way toward the busy intersection I knew I would have to cross, I felt more confident with each step. I was also able to make out some structures that reinforced my sense of direction.

I reached the corner where our small side street met Don Mills Road, which was less active in the evening but still had enough traffic that a person had to be careful getting across (six lanes to cross; three in each direction). From my vantage point on the southeast corner of the intersection, I could see the traffic signals. Although I couldn't read the symbols on the "walk" and "don't walk" lights, I was able to tell the difference between the orange "don't walk" and the white "walk" signals. If I focused my gaze on the signal I could also see when it changed. I made it all the way across the six lanes of asphalt! Once across, I set off to find my landmark —a white, wooden sign with black lettering that I knew would be positioned next to the driveway where I would need to turn in.

I found the sign a few minutes later. Just to be sure, I walked right up to it and tried to make out the words. What a relief it was to be able to just walk down the driveway of my workplace. I was truly succeeding this time. With a swipe of my security pass, I walked into the station and climbed the stairs to the third floor. At the far end of the hall was the master control room where I knew I would find Cindy. She was surprised to see me walk in and asked how I got there. I looked down, pointed at my feet and said, "With these!" I could tell from her body language she was not happy with me, but she knew as well as I did that I'm the type of person who has to test his boundaries now and then.

The mobility worker's first visit to the condo was the following week and, after showing me the cane, we went to the stairwell of our building, so I could get a feel for using it on the stairs. She made another appointment for the following week so we could go for a walk and talk about getting across intersections with lights and without.

On that next appointment, I didn't use the cane and she didn't ask me to use it. I wanted to show her how I got around without the cane, and I think she wanted to see that, too.

As I explained to her, my "large vision" was pretty good up to about twenty metres. I was able to see where I was walking well enough not to bump into people or objects, and most of the time I could see changes in the walking surface well enough not to trip on them.

One thing I did have to learn about my new-found state of vision was that, with my upper peripheral vision being basically gone, I had to train myself not to walk with my head down. That took some doing. When I first started walking around on my own, the natural instinct was to look down more so I could see where I was walking, but without my upper peripheral vision, I could not see things coming at me. On a few occasions, I nearly walked directly into people or sign posts. After about an hour, the mobility worker felt I had a pretty good handle on getting around and, until I needed her for something else, she was going to close my file.

The next time I took a walk on my own, I went over to a nearby shopping mall about a 15-minute walk from home. Cane in hand, I set off on my journey. I arrived at the mall without incident and made my way to my favourite place in the food court to get a bite to eat. Walking through the mall was fairly easy and even at the food court, I didn't have any challenges moving around the tables or other shoppers. Reading the menu board at my chosen location was virtually impossible, but I had been there enough times to know what I wanted to buy. From there, I walked to the corner store, where I got my first taste of most retailers' responses to the cane. I walked up and asked the clerk if she could show me where to find a bottle of root beer. She didn't speak much English and didn't seem to know what root beer was, but when I mentioned a few brand names, she sprang into action. She was off like a shot to pick one out of the cooler for me. I thought to myself, now that's good customer service! From there, I headed home, my trip complete and feeling really good about the day. When I got home, I called Cindy at work to tell her about my mission. Even without seeing her face, through the phone I could tell she was almost bursting with pride at what I had done. I've said it before and I'll say it again — it was great to have such a fantastic cheerleader on my side.

Two days before Christmas 2005, I decided to pick up some orange juice, since the stores were going to be closed for the holidays. Cindy was sleeping during the day in preparation for her next midnight shift,

Life's Not Over, It Just Looks Different

so it was time for another trip on my own. I walked into the grocery store, found the juice aisle and began to read the labels as well as I could. I didn't have a good magnifying glass yet, so this wasn't an easy task. I was having difficulty reading the packages and, although there were lots of people around, no one asked if I needed any help. To be fair, I didn't ask for any help, either. This was a test for me to see what I could do for myself. After a few minutes, I found juice, but it wasn't exactly what I wanted; it was an orange, banana, strawberry blend. I was tired of looking and it wasn't awful, so I just bought it.

A couple of days after Christmas, I was back in the same store because I had only purchased one carton of juice on the previous trip. Once again, it took me a few minutes of reading the labels up close, and when I say "up close" I mean right to my nose, but this time I found exactly what I wanted — pure orange juice, not a blend. I walked out of the store feeling very good about what I had done. The mission was a complete success, and I gained another little piece of my independence.

FRIENDS

Losing my sight showed me that I have the greatest friends and family anyone could wish for. I had friends and co-workers visit me in the hospital without any prompting, and many more sent flowers, cards and one of the biggest surprises — a basket of chocolate!

I was particularly touched by the basket and accompanying card from my former co-workers in Winnipeg. I hadn't worked in Winnipeg for more than seven years, and yet nearly every one of my co-workers from those days had signed the card. It was overwhelming to receive their gift and good wishes. When I called to say thank you, I spoke to the man who headed up the collection and he told me that even after they sent the package, some people were still finding out about what happened to me and wanted to chip in. I was even more touched.

As a way of saying thank you and also to give them some indication of what my reading level looked like, I typed up thank you notes in 48-point font. I could've saved paper by resizing the font down to a more common size, but I wanted to let everyone know how much my sight had been affected. I also felt by keeping the note in that font size, they'd know it was written by me, and not by someone else on my behalf.

A few friends did not find out about the surgery until I began sending out email updates on my progress to family and friends. One of my go-kart racing buddies was among that group. He replied to the email saying he was "gutted" by the news and would call me in a few days. On the phone a few days later, I reassured him, as I had everyone else, that the doctor said the loss was temporary and we had to wait to see what I'd get back.

Less than two months after leaving the hospital, it was time to do some Christmas shopping. Cindy and I were able to shop together for our nephew and nieces, but when it came to shopping for Cindy, I was in a pickle. How was I going to shop for her and still keep the element of surprise on Christmas morning? Our friend Kim mentioned she was going shopping the next day, so the three of us went to the mall together and, once there, Cindy went one way while Kim and I went another. In less than an hour, I checked two things off my list for Cindy. I had two more stores to check out, but they weren't in that mall. Kim told me she was going to another mall in a few days and would take me along, so I might finish my shopping there. Perfect!

After the shopping trip with Kim at the second mall, I still had one more thing on my list for Cindy, which I was pretty sure I could find at the mall near home. More than just a gift, however, it was another test of my abilities. In the mall, after asking at the customer service desk, another shopper overheard our conversation and offered to take me to the store I was searching for. The mall, however, was being renovated and we couldn't find it. She dropped me off at a similar store, only to return moments later, because she'd found the one I'd been looking for and again offered to take me there. I thanked her once again, not only for taking the time to help me but for coming back to get me. I got the item I was shopping for, and my list was complete!

We didn't send out any Christmas cards that year, so I decided to email everyone I could to wish them a Merry Christmas and give them an update on my progress — in 36-point font, down from the 48-point font a few weeks earlier. I thanked everyone for being so wonderful and wrote how lucky I was to have such great people around me. One friend responded saying that he was just thinking how unlucky I was, until he read my email. It's all about perspective.

Trying to get back on script

I spent a lot of time in my school years behind a microphone recording demo tapes and trying to hone my skills as an announcer. Once I got into television, the dream of being a voice on the air was put on hold. It never really died; it just slipped further and further to the back of my mind as my television career grew. In 2004, I thought it was time to breathe new life into the dream, but with a twist. Rather than trying to get into radio, I discovered the world of freelance voice work.

I started by taking voice workshops and eventually produced a demo CD I felt was professional enough to shop around to the various agencies looking for freelancers.

During the workshops, it was suggested I should look for opportunities to be in a studio environment, honing my skills and gaining experience. My search led me to VoicePrint, a non-profit reading service for the vision impaired and print-restricted. I joined them as a volunteer reader shortly after completing my first series of voice workshops.

In the summer of 2005, after reading for VoicePrint for almost a year, I was approached by the program manager about reading a show for their national service. The proposed show would feature stories from a variety of newspapers in Manitoba and Saskatchewan. She knew I had lived in those areas and thought I would have a good sense of the material and for stories that would be of interest to the listeners. I jumped at the chance for the increased responsibility. She told me I'd be responsible for gathering enough material for two half hour episodes each week to air Saturdays and Sundays. The show was basically mine to put together, voice and produce each week.

By September 2005, I had voiced the first few episodes of the new show on VoicePrint, had signed with a talent agency and even had a few auditions.

Then October hit — pain, surgery and vision loss.

I wasn't going to just give up on my dream, though. A couple of weeks after leaving the hospital, I was determined to get back to reading scripts so I wouldn't lose too much ground on everything I had done getting my voice career started. I knew I wasn't ready to read full programs for VoicePrint yet, but I thought short scripts might be okay. The voice agency I had signed with often sent scripts by email for performers to record as an audition at home and send back as an MP3 file. Recording at home was a good thing for me in the early days of my recovery, because I could print the scripts I was sent in whatever font size I was comfortable with. Cindy and I bought a good quality microphone and audio software so I could record in the comfort of my own home at any time of day.

The staff at VoicePrint had been checking in with Cindy for updates on my recovery, so we decided to stop by and say hello. During that visit I had a chat with the program manager about reading some short pieces because I wanted to stay involved. The first thing she started sending me to read were promos for their weekly interview program. I recorded them at home each week and emailed the MP3 files back for her to air. A few months later, I started reading one news article a week, usually about five minutes in length, that was added to a program with a collection of articles from other parts of Toronto. It felt good to be involved again.

Sometimes the five-minute articles took an hour or more to produce, partly because I was very picky about how it sounded, but also because, no matter what font size I used, sometimes my brain still had trouble taking in the words on the pages. I didn't want the people at VoicePrint to know it was taking me so long to do one story, so recording from home allowed me to keep that secret. No matter how long it took to get it done, all they heard was the finished product and they liked it, so everyone was happy.

I didn't tell the agency about the surgery or my sight loss right away, because they weren't sending me any scripts to audition. Once they did start sending me scripts, I still didn't feel I had to tell them, because thanks to the Internet, I was able to record the scripts at home and email an MP3 file back to them, as well.

I finally told them about three months after the surgery when they sent me an email for a live audition I was to attend. I told them the short version of what had happened to my sight and asked if I could get a copy of the script in large print. They said it'd be no problem. As a courtesy, they also sent me a copy of the script, so I printed it off and practised all week before the audition.

On the day of the audition, I met the producers, who handed me their large-print version of the script. Mine was larger, so I chose to read from it instead. The audition did not go well at all. Auditioning live for the first time in my life and probably some insecurity about how well I would manage with my large print script made for a bad combination.

I took my spot behind the microphone alongside the other actors in the room. We would act out the script as an ensemble, each of us doing our part. I bumbled my way through it, sometimes missing cues and losing the flow of the scene. At one point, when I missed my cue, one of the actors tried to help me out by telling me what page we were on.

The producer piped up and said, "No, his script is different." For the next scene, only I and one of the female actors were needed, so the others left. The producers asked if I was going to be able to do it. I said I'd try, but it didn't go well. I got very flustered and had to stop. The producers said they thought they had enough of my voice on tape to judge my audition and thanked me for coming in. As I left the studio with the producer, she asked one of the other male actors to go into the studio and help finish the scene.

I felt defeated and embarrassed. It was my first live audition for the agency and it was a disaster. I really wanted to make a go of the voice business, and now it looked like that was just not going to happen.

On the 90-minute trip home, I kicked myself for trying to do something I obviously wasn't ready for. I was afraid the agency was going to be mad at me for showing up to the audition when I knew I wasn't able to do the work. Strangely, I never heard a word about the audition from the agency.

Seven weeks later, I received an email, then a phone call, and another phone call, from one of my friends at Global who was passing on a message. The agency really wanted to get in touch with me. They wanted to book me, not just for an audition, but an actual recording session — my first gig! I was very nervous and excited, but eager to do it. The negative experience of the previous audition crossed my mind, but I convinced myself enough time had passed and I felt better now than when I went into the earlier audition. I asked the agency to request a large-print copy of the script, in at least 36-point font.

At the studio, the producer handed me a script and asked if it was large enough. I said no, and he printed off a larger version. It was larger, but not really large enough. Not wanting to be seen as difficult, I told him I thought I could work with it. That was a mistake. I tried reading the script a few times, but kept stumbling and losing my place on the page. The producer finally stopped me, saying it just wasn't going to work. He was right.

As we walked out of the studio, he tried to console me a little, telling me that he wouldn't say anything nasty about me to the agency and that he would see if I could still be paid a little bit of money for my time. He walked me to an exit and held the door for me to leave.

Once outside, I realized it wasn't the same door I had entered through. I stood there for a moment trying to figure out which way I should walk. I was in an area of the city I didn't know very well, and with less eyesight it took a while to get my bearings. I knew I couldn't just stand there, so I picked a direction and started walking. I soon realized I had been let out just around the corner from the main entrance. Just like after the last session, I felt terrible, drained of energy. I called a cab from my cell phone and went home.

This time, I thought, I really needed to stop fooling myself. I obviously wasn't ready to record any sessions, and it was time to face up to that fact. To make matters worse, I felt like I had embarrassed myself and the agency. That producer was annoyed, and certainly this time the agency was going to hear about it from him. This wasn't just an audition; it was a gig and I had left them in the lurch.

When I got home, I emailed the agency to tell them that I did not appear to be as ready to do this work as I thought I was and I recommended they pull me from their roster. One of the agents replied to my email asking if I was still recovering, expected to recover, or if my sight loss was now permanent. I told him I would know better the following week when I saw the ophthalmologist.

Rather than pulling me from the roster altogether, the agency put me on the sidelines, listing me as "unavailable until further notice" on the website. A few days later however, when I went back to the website, I discovered they had pulled me off the list completely. I was disappointed, but not surprised. The ironic thing about the recording session: the script I'd been given was to voice over a commercial for an optician.

BUREAUCRACY

Prior to October 2005, I had never given much thought to the short-term and long-term disability components of our health benefits package at work. Once thrown into it, I learned not only how valuable the programs are, but also discovered first-hand how much bureaucracy can be involved.

The short-term disability portion of the plan was basically painless. There was no interruption to my bi-weekly pay cycle, and I was pleased to find that our short-term disability plan covered 100 per cent of my salary while I was in hospital and then recovering at home.

The company's short-term disability plan lasted 90 days, which covered what the insurance industry calls the "elimination period" for long-term disability. This meant there would be no interruption of income for me — that is, as long as the paperwork was all completed on time. This is when the fun started.

The long-term disability (LTD) plan provided 70 per cent of my earnings. The most important part of that was that the long-term benefits were not taxed, as I had been paying for the coverage as part of my benefits package. The short-term disability pay, by contrast, was subject to the usual payroll deductions and taxes. The LTD benefits could last up to three years, and then the insurance company would assess my condition to see if I could return to work in some form or be considered permanently disabled. I was pretty sure I would recover long before the three years were up, but because the neurosurgeon and ophthalmologist said to give it a year to see how much I'd recovered, I knew I'd be on disability for at least that long.

I went on short-term disability at the end of October and was expected to be on it until the end of January, when the switch to long-term disability would occur. As the end of January neared, Cindy's and my stress levels began to rise. At the request of the insurance company, I gave the neurosurgeon a form to fill out to verify that I was indeed eligible for LTD benefits. As the deadline approached, the neurosurgeon had not filled out his portion of the paperwork. The case worker from the insurance company was not willing to view the original doctor's note as enough evidence to start the claim and was pressuring me to get the paperwork signed by the doctor. She did tell me that if I was able to get her some current eye test results, then she could use that to start the claim. With that in mind, I was on the phone that day to get the latest eye test results. I had done a visual field test at the hospital earlier in the month, but had not received a call back with the results, so I decided to make an appointment with my optometrist. The last time I had seen him was sometime before the surgery, and I figured if he could do the visual field and acuity tests, his word would be good since he'd been looking after my sight for the past four years.

The optometrist told me things about my vision that I had not even heard from the doctors at the hospital. We first spoke over the phone, and during that conversation, the optometrist said what I was describing to him sounded like agnosia. We made an appointment for

Life's Not Over, It Just Looks Different

the next day, so he could examine me in person. After we hung up, I searched online for information about agnosia. Agnosia, I discovered, is an inability to recognize things like shapes, faces or even colours. This description sounded very much like what I was experiencing, but I was disheartened to read that there was no known cure and, although one can recover, a full recovery was unlikely — not the news I wanted.

When I saw him the next day, the optometrist gave me a different diagnosis. After examining me, he said I had a condition called cortical blindness, meaning the eyes were fine, but the brain was not processing what the eyes were giving it. That made a lot of sense to me, because I was able to see people and make out some of their facial features, but I wasn't able to make that last bit of recognition that allowed me to identify someone without hearing him or her speak. Walking through the mall or on the sidewalk, people were basically just 3-D silhouettes to me. I also noticed that when I looked around a room, I felt as though there was a thin black screen over everything I was seeing. In our living room, we had a tall halogen lamp with a 300-watt bulb that gave off plenty of light. In the evening, however, I had to check the switch to see if the light had been turned all the way up, because the room still seemed dark to me.

During the visit to the optometrist, he performed the standard eye tests, including having me read the letters on the eye chart to check my acuity. He started with the very top line which only had one letter on it.

"I think that's a big E on the top of the chart, but it's fuzzy to me," I said.

"If you can't see that one, you're messed up," he quipped. He wrote a note for me to give to the insurance company saying he had examined me and determined my visual acuity to be 20/200 — legally blind.

A short time later, I sent the optometrist's note to the case worker at the insurance company. It was sufficient to start the claim. She told me she wasn't surprised I found a way to get her the information she needed.

"I knew you'd get it done," she said.

Finally, I received a call from the neurosurgeon's office late in the week telling me he had filled out the forms and they were going in the mail the next day. I guess all my phone calls and heartfelt pleas to his receptionist paid off. Just call me the squeaky wheel!

A few weeks before going on long-term disability, I had tried without success to start a discussion about what else I might be able to do at my current workplace, or if they would at least let me test out what I could or couldn't do in my master control job. It wasn't until the LTD kicked in, though, that discussions actually started about how to get me back to work. The insurance company phoned within days of the LTD starting, and we talked about that. I told the case worker the folks at work were unsure of the process and who needed to initiate that. She told me she was the one and that I should make a call to my boss to see about doing some job shadowing to assess what I could see and do related to the day-to-day operations of master control.

Life's Not Over, It Just Looks Different

The last week of February, I went in to spend the day job shadowing as the insurance company requested. It was the first time since losing my sight that I was officially allowed to get my hands on the equipment at work and … myself. There were three different master control … was to try out all three over … different in each room. I … uipment, since it was the way … ne least experience in, and I … er after having been away for … eks of training, I had only … nt before going into the

… of the job with little problem or … There were other tasks I was able to do, too, like reading the CRTC[1] logs, with the aid of my hand-held magnifier, but I was slow at it because the magnifier's field of vision was so small. At one point in the experiment, I was trying to read a page sent down by another department asking for changes to the log. I was having trouble reading the page and, try as I might, the words just weren't making sense. It took more than a minute for me to realize the page was upside down, which amused my co-worker.

---

[1] The CRTC is the Canadian Radio-Television and Telecommunications Commission, Canada's broadcast regulator.

Mom/Dad:

I got Chris to sign his book for you.

Love

Jim

The high volume of paperwork master control received each day was part of the reason for doing the shadowing. If we found I could do the job well enough, aided by devices like a CCTV for the paperwork, then perhaps I could get back to work and off disability. Overall, I was disappointed with the way the shadowing went. I was really hoping I could have walked into master control and slipped right back into the role with the aid of some assistive technology.

Later, in a conversation with my co-worker and manager, both told me I was able to see and do more than they had expected. It was nice to have the boss impressed with what I could do, but at the same time it taught me something about the state of my vision loss. I learned that once people heard I was vision impaired, they often assumed it meant a near-total or even total vision loss. On the upside, I suppose it was a good feeling to surprise them with what I could do, but I think in some cases it meant I was held back from things because of the perception of my abilities. By the end of the shift, I had a terrible headache that I attributed to staring too long and concentrating hard on everything I was trying to see.

Two days later, I went in again to work in one of the older master control rooms for more perspective on my abilities. Part way through the shift, after having tried all I wanted to do that was different from the previous day's test, I went into an empty office and sat at a computer to type a report of everything I was able to do and see over the day and a half. I gave one copy of it to my boss for his records, one to the insurance company and took one to the doctor, whom I was scheduled to see the next day. The neurosurgeon was given another form by the insurance company that they wanted him to fill out once he had seen me and assessed my abilities. Based on that form they wanted a determination by the doctor on whether or not I could return to work at my job or not.

CURVE BALL

On the first day of March 2006, Cindy and I received a phone call at home asking us both to attend a staff meeting at 8:30 a.m. the next morning.

Just prior to taking that call, Cindy and I had watched a show on the business channel about work-related topics. One of the featured segments in the program was how to tell when you are about to be let go from your job. The guest on the show said if you're called into a meeting and there is a person from human resources in a room adjacent to your meeting, or in the room where you are having the meeting, that's a pretty good sign you're about to be let go. Cindy and I joked about how ironic it would be if that was the subject of the meeting the next day.

I was just about to leave for the station when the insurance company called to tell me that a new case worker would be taking over my file and that she would call the HR department at work to let them know. I smiled and told her I was about to leave for a meeting at work and there's a good chance the HR person will be there.

"Oh, no!" she said, obviously concerned. "Call me later and let me know what happened in the meeting."

Life's Not Over, It Just Looks Different

At the station, most of our co-workers were there, buzzing with anticipation. We filed into the studio where the meeting was taking place with some of our friends.

"What do you think this is all about?" one of them wondered out loud.

"I'll let you know," I joked. "I'm actually the one that called the meeting. I'm just waiting for everyone to take their seats." As Cindy looked around the room, she saw one of the HR reps in the back corner of the studio. We simultaneously gave each other a knowing look. At that point, we were pretty sure we knew what was going to happen next.

After a short wait, the VP of our department walked to the front of the room. The chairs had been arranged in two sections, five rows deep, with four chairs on either side of a wide aisle between them. The VP stared straight down the centre aisle, avoiding eye contact with any of the staff as he informed us that in six months our jobs would be eliminated and that master control for all stations in the network would be run by the Calgary facility. He went on to say that there would be some positions created in Calgary to cover the increased workload and we were welcome to apply. He then handed the meeting over to the HR director, who told us about the severance package and fielded questions from the staff. With the bad news delivered, the meeting broke up a short time later. In a conversation with the HR director afterward, he told me that as long as I was on disability I could not be laid off and my disability benefits were secure. He added that if I was declared fit to return to work, then I would get a letter spelling out my severance like everyone else. I felt like I was at a big disadvantage, because I would be looking for a job in broadcasting somewhere else but with limited eyesight — a definite drawback that would give my co-workers a leg up if we applied for the same jobs.

"I'm not sure what the other stations in town will want with a half-blind master control operator," I said.

"Listen," he said. "Apply anyway. If you can prove to them you can do the job, they'll jump at the chance to have you on staff. You'll beef up their employment equity numbers." I found it odd that he didn't say anything about my current workplace trying to keep me. Wouldn't I be good for their employment equity numbers, too? The question crossed my mind, but I didn't ask it out loud. We were all in shock as we left the meeting.

At home, Cindy was the first to shed a few tears over the news. She's a strong lady, but in the privacy of our own home, she was safe to let her feelings out. I put my arms around her and we held each other tight while she sobbed into my shoulder. The layoff notice we had just received meant we were both going to be out of a job in six months. Although I wasn't handed a letter outlining a severance package that day, Cindy got a letter, so for her, the layoff was very real at that moment. She regained her composure after a couple of minutes, and we sat down facing each other from either end of the couch and got into a conversation about our options going forward. We discussed looking for new jobs and even the possibility of this being our cue to move out of Toronto. Perhaps we'd apply for jobs in Calgary or maybe even move back home to Winnipeg to be closer to family. We spent most of the day talking about the possibilities, even though she was supposed to be sleeping because she had to work again that night at midnight. But as she said to me, after news like that, who could sleep? She was absolutely right.

That afternoon, I had an appointment with the neurosurgeon. He did a few simple tests to check my sight and asked a few questions about how I felt, aside from my eyesight. He told me point blank that I was clearly legally blind and qualified as disabled. He quickly moved on to discuss the form the insurance company had sent him for a progress update. We talked about the job shadowing, and I gave him a copy of my report, which he asked me to explain further. When I gave him a bit more perspective on what I was able to do and see at work, he said it was unlikely I'd be able to return to work in a master control setting, but I appeared healthy and could function well enough with my sight the way it was to do some other job with the aid of a CCTV unit or software for the computer.

That's when I told him about the layoff notice we had just received and how I was now in a tight spot. I told him straight up I did not want him to fudge any reports to keep me on disability. In fact, I told him, I would rather he told them I was able to return to work in some form. Truth was, I was bored and wanted to get back in the game, even if it meant being taken off disability and facing the layoff notice with Cindy and our co-workers.

The shock of being told I wouldn't be able to go back to my job in master control didn't really sink in until after I left his office. It hadn't been the full year we were supposed to wait before making final decisions about my progress. In fact, it was only a little over four months into my recovery and already he was starting to close the door. How could this be? What happened to waiting a year? Had he given up hope? Was I not recovering as quickly as he'd hoped? Or was the idea of waiting a year really his way of not breaking the bad news to me right from the start? I had so many questions and yet didn't know how to articulate them at that moment in his office. On the other hand, my progress had not been moving nearly as fast as I hoped, so I think in the back of my mind I was starting to realize I would never get my full sight back. I wasn't ready to face that reality yet, so it hurt to hear it from him. Working in broadcasting was all I'd ever wanted to do.

The other problem was that I didn't have a back-up plan. I've always felt better about things in general when I know that there's a plan B. This time I was caught off guard. I had been focusing on trying to get better. I was forcing myself to read smaller and smaller print almost every day, which seemed to be working. I was out for walks, gaining more and more of my independence, but now this.

Cindy and I had talked about "what if" scenarios in case I didn't recover my sight, but those plans weren't ready and I wasn't ready to leave TV yet. It slowly dawned on me that, between the layoff notice earlier in the day and the doctor's reality check for me that afternoon, perhaps I wasn't meant to stay in TV.

Life's Not Over, It Just Looks Different

Later that evening we got a couple of phone calls from friends in other departments who had heard the news and then a call from a co-worker who was not taking the news of his layoff very well. Cindy and I both talked to him for a while before Cindy left for work.

Around 1 a.m. I fell asleep watching television and when I woke up about an hour later, I decided to go to bed for the night. But I couldn't sleep. I just stared at the ceiling, everything that had happened that day cycling through my brain, over and over. Suddenly, I sat up in bed. A horrible realization dawned on me: I was going to be laid off at some point, probably before getting any more of my sight back, and I was going out into the job search world with a disadvantage I had never faced before. It was too much for me. I cried, harder than I had cried in a long time. I called Cindy at work, and right away she knew I had finally cracked from the events of the day. She got someone to cover for her, so she could bring me to work so I wouldn't be alone.

When she walked in a few minutes later, I was getting worse. I was crying uncontrollably and shaking all over; my neck and shoulders were tightening up and I was starting to hyperventilate. Cindy helped me get to the car and, as we drove away from the condo, I continued to cry and was gasping for air. She changed her mind about our destination.

"I'm taking you to the hospital, instead," she said. "I think you're having a panic attack."

At the hospital, after talking to the triage nurse I was put in the "quiet room," away from the others in the main waiting area. I sat on a chair in that room for a minute or two, but my neck and shoulders were so tight, sitting was not an option. I slid down to the carpeted floor and lay there in the fetal position for about two hours. The problem was twofold: I went from being upset about the announcement of the job loss and the prospect of trying to find a new job with less eyesight; to being scared because there were times when I couldn't catch my breath, even as I was trying to calm down.

Two hours went by in the quiet room, and slowly I began to relax and speak in more coherent sentences with Cindy, who had been by my side the whole time. I stayed there for another hour or so and once I was able to sit up, figuring I had myself back under control, I told Cindy I wanted to go home.

The entire time I was in the quiet room, no doctors or nurses ever came in to check on me. As we walked out, we told the triage nurse (a different one than when we checked in) that we were leaving. She had no idea who we were.

"Were you told about us being in the quiet room?" Cindy asked.

"They told me someone was in there, but didn't tell me who," the nurse replied.

I told the nurse I felt calm enough to go home, where I was going to take a sleeping pill and call my psychiatrist in the morning and we left. I have no idea why the emergency doctor didn't come in to see me, but I learned many months later that the hospital didn't have any crisis staff on shift after 11 p.m., so there was no one there for me to talk to anyway.

I saw the psychiatrist later that afternoon to tell him all that had happened the previous day, including the visit to the hospital. He said our reaction to the layoff news was perfectly normal and that even my panic was normal because I had been through a lot in the past four months.

THE BUREAUCRACY CONTINUES

The day after, I called the case worker at the insurance company about my LTD claim. I told her what happened at the staff meeting the day before. She said she found it odd that I didn't get a letter explaining my severance like the others and told me she would be talking to her HR contact later in the day to find out more.

I called human resources myself that afternoon and asked if the doctor reports that I can go back to work, would I be taken off disability and then receive a letter like Cindy and our co-workers had? She said I would, but she added they were going to do their best to make sure I was not left out in the cold with no money. She told me she had not spoken to the insurance company yet, so she wasn't sure why I was getting a new case worker or any other details on that matter.

The following week, I called the new case worker to introduce myself.

"Have you received the doctor's report yet?" I asked. She had not.

"I have a copy of it with me if you'd like a copy," I told her. She asked me to fax it to her.

About an hour after I sent the fax, she called to say she'd received it and had looked over my case.

"How do you feel about going back to work?" she asked.

Life's Not Over, It Just Looks Different

"I'm eager to get off disability, because I am bored out of my tree! But there are parts of the job I'm still not able to do."

"Are you feeling pressured to get back to work so you can go to Calgary if there's a position open?"

"I do feel like I'm in a tight spot," I said. "But I don't want to rush back only to fail and have the folks at work upset and feeling like I returned too early."

She said a rehabilitation worker would have to assess my ability to return to work and that someone would call me to set up an appointment the following week.

Two weeks later, I learned there was a job posting for a supervisory position in Calgary. I read the description of the job and felt I could do it with the aid of a CCTV unit and magnifying software. The following day, I called the case worker to ask if I was allowed to apply for the posting, thinking it was better to ask before doing anything that might negatively affect my disability benefits.

"If you think you are up to it and able to do the job, then go ahead and apply," she said.

"Will applying for the job cause my benefits to stop?" She said no.

"Have you received a call from the rehabilitation worker yet?" she asked.

"Not yet."

She said she'd have her call me and we could go over the posting to see what adjustments might need to be made in order for me to do the job.

Having been given the go ahead to return to work in some form, I was eager to do just that, which had me wondering how I would approach interviews as a vision impaired person. I wanted a fair shot at any job I applied for and to show my ability and desire for the job, without too much focus on my lack of sight. I had no intention of applying for a job I could not do.

I didn't really know how my sight would be viewed in an interview, but based on the reactions from some people who seemed to think vision impaired meant total sight loss, I was racking my brain trying to find a way to put a positive spin on the situation. I ran through different scenarios in my head, but I wasn't going to know for sure until I actually had an interview. I didn't know many vision impaired people at that point, so I didn't have any personal connections to draw upon that I felt would fully understand my concerns. Even the case worker had given an evasive answer. She couldn't answer, she wasn't sure, but she didn't even have a vague idea of where to go for assistance.

Ten minutes after speaking with the case worker, the rehabilitation worker at the insurance company called. She asked if I had a copy of the posting so we could go over it together to see what it would require,

Life's Not Over, It Just Looks Different

and we set up a time to meet the following week. Being given the go ahead to apply for this job was very exciting. It meant I was going to try and get back to work. It meant I might be able to stay in my chosen career. The prospect of moving to Calgary added to the excitement. I had visited Calgary many times and thought it would be great to live there someday, if the right opportunity came along.

I set to work right away, getting my résumé and cover letter ready. Time was running late on the posting, so I couldn't wait for the meeting with the rehabilitation worker before applying.

Early in April 2006, less than a month after the VP of our department had dropped a bombshell on the entire staff at a group meeting, the HR person called me to say a plan had been devised to help me get back to work. All parties involved would meet to discuss the plan within a few weeks, but only after my boss was able to get the software I needed to do the job. I told her I was going to contact him about getting a CCTV to do the paperwork as well. Once the software and the CCTV were in place, we could have a meaningful discussion about getting me back to work, but until then, I had to sit tight. She went on to say that under the current insurance policy, when the job came to an end and everything moved to Calgary at the end of August, I would trigger a "recurrence" clause and go back on disability rather than being laid off, because the time line to the layoff would be less than six months after I returned to the job.

A few days later, it was the insurance company's turn to call. The rehabilitation worker confirmed basically everything I had heard from the HR person. She also said my workplace was working on getting the software. I told her I called my boss to tell him I needed a CCTV, as well. Due to the short time frame involved, however, the company might not pay for the CCTV, and the insurance company likely wouldn't either. I knew of a government program that helped people with disabilities, and I asked if the insurer would refund my portion of the cost. She said that was much more reasonable and that they likely would cover that much. The other option, she said, was to try and rent a CCTV for the few months I would need it.

I didn't hear from the insurance company again until mid-May when the rehabilitation worker called to ask me how my inquiry with the CNIB went about finding a CCTV. She had been unable to find one to rent, and the insurer was not willing to pay the cost for such a short time. She said she asked the HR person at work if there was any way they could help get a job for me either in Toronto or Calgary.

"I'm actually working on that myself," I said. "I've applied for jobs in two different departments here in Toronto."

"Have you been applying anywhere outside of your current employer?" she asked.

"I do have one application pending for a completely different company," I said.

Life's Not Over, It Just Looks Different

So, despite the doctor's view that I wouldn't likely be able to return to master control, a plan was still being considered to get me back to work in that role. I had mixed feelings about this. If I was sure I could be just as good at the job as I had been before, aided by the software and a CCTV, that would be great. If not though, and the doctor's opinion was correct, I felt my actions to seek out and apply for other roles I could do was the more productive approach.

PLOTTING NEW DIRECTIONS

Even before being told by the neurosurgeon in early March that I likely wouldn't go back to my position in master control, I think in some ways I was starting to realize it for myself. From the start of the new year up to that day in the doctor's office, Cindy and I had occasionally discussed what life after master control might look like, if needed.

One idea we tossed around a few times was that my time in broadcasting didn't have to end, that perhaps I could do something administrative or even a management position if I could find one. That way, my 15 years of experience wouldn't go to waste and I wouldn't have to start a new career completely from scratch.

We decided it might be good to take some courses to bolster my skills and put me in a better position for an office job in the broadcast world. With the doctor's opinion that I could get back to work in some form, I was eager to do so and if I could find a new role without having to wait for the insurance company and my workplace to come up with something for me, that would be great.

I'm at my happiest when I have more than one thing on the go. While living in Winnipeg, I had my job at the television station and on the side I was either taking courses or operating a small business re-stocking candy in vending machines around the city. In Toronto, when I wasn't doing my regular job, I was doing volunteer work. Part of the time, I was looking at job websites for positions in the broadcast industry I thought I could do with reduced sight. Other times, I was looking at courses, checking out offerings from the colleges and universities in the Toronto area.

In the midst of all that, I got a call from the CNIB, asking if I was still interested in learning braille. After a short chat with the rehabilitation worker, we decided that grade 1 braille was all I would really need. Grade 1 braille is all the letters of the alphabet, the numbers 0–9 and some punctuation. At that point, roughly three months after the surgery, I was able to read large fonts, and, with the help of a CCTV unit, I could read smaller printed materials. The idea was that the braille would come in handy in elevators or for marking my CDs since I had trouble reading what they were. The rehabilitation worker and I set up a time for her to come to our condo for the first lesson.

Before starting the braille lessons, I was given a brochure called "The Six Magic Dots of Braille." "Magic" is a very good term for it. When I first got the pamphlet, I felt the dots on it and thought, "There's no way I'm going to learn this." Once I started the lessons, however, the thought of reading by dots became less daunting. Having the bi-weekly lessons in a one-on-one setting in my own home also made for a much more relaxed learning environment. For each appointment, the rehabilitation worker — who had less sight than I did — was driven by a CNIB volunteer to our building and then picked up an hour later by the same person.

The pattern of the dots that make up the letters and numbers is actually quite simple and logical. The real learning for me came in the tactile exercises. From a very young age we learn about the world by touching things, and braille is no different. The fingers do the reading where the eyes cannot. When I told a friend who worked closely with the vision impaired community what I was doing, she told me only seven per cent of the vision impaired population is able to read braille. I was surprised to hear the number was so low, and at the same time, it made me feel kind of special to be part of such a small group.

Two months after starting the braille lessons, my instructor retired. I liked working with her because she was more than a helpful resource; she was also a sympathetic and supportive ear as I learned how to be a vision impaired person.

The second week of March, I had the first lesson with my new teacher, and we continued the arrangement I'd had with the previous instructor. She came to my home rather than me having to go somewhere for the lesson. The new instructor was sighted and therefore had a different approach in our lessons. What stood out most to me at first was watching her read the workbook or the assignments she gave me. Being sighted, she was able to look at the dots on the page without touching them. I teased her about it on the first day, telling her that was cheating. I was told right from the start that if I could see the dots, there was no point in teaching me braille. Luckily (or unluckily) my sight was just poor enough that I could see dots on the page but not with enough definition to read them.

Life's Not Over, It Just Looks Different

The new teacher, who tolerated my teasing very well, was fun to work with. When I needed to give my fingers a rest from all the reading, what I referred to as "braille finger," she told me how she came to be a rehabilitation worker and what it was like learning grades 1 and 2 braille in her college classes. Although I'd never given it much thought, the idea that I could approach this as I would any other course I might take was comforting. My day-to-day recovery wasn't always enjoyable, but the times that I could sit back and look at it as a learning experience made it much easier to take.

In mid-March, two months after beginning the search for what my work life might look like if I didn't stay in television, I enrolled in the Canadian Securities Course (CSC). The CSC is a home study course, which meant I could do it on my own time and I didn't have to find my way to a classroom or campus somewhere in the city, at least not until it came time to write the exams. I was given one year to complete the course, which consisted of digesting the material in two textbooks, with an exam to write after each book. I still didn't know what my next job might be or if I was changing careers at all, but I thought it would be good to have something to focus on while I was off work. Even if I didn't use what I learned professionally, the knowledge would be helpful in looking after my own investments.

Choosing to enroll in the CSC, which to many of my friends and family seemed to come out of left field for a guy who had worked in broadcasting for so long, was actually not the big stretch it appeared to be. Although broadcasting was my chosen career, investing and finance was something that had captured my attention in my early twenties when a couple of my co-workers suggested I open an RRSP. I followed their advice and found an advisor to help me start saving a small amount every month.

Over the years, my interest grew as I learned more about different investments. Once a week, I went to the laundromat near my apartment to wash my clothes and, since I had about 90 minutes to kill, I read the business section of the newspaper, piquing my interest even more. By 2006, when I decided to enroll in the CSC, I had been investing for more than ten years, so I was just building on what I already knew.

I wrote the first of the two CSC exams in September 2006. I had booked the exam weeks earlier and told them I needed some accommodations to read the test. They asked for a doctor's note, which I provided, and the administrators said they would have no problem meeting my needs for the exam and told me when and where to write the test. The day before the exam, I had a friend help me read a map, so I could find the location and the best way to get there by transit. We determined the best subway stop for me to get there and I felt reasonably confident I could find the location myself.

The day of the exam I left home 90 minutes before the test was scheduled to start. I knew it would only take about 45 minutes to get to the location itself, but I wanted to give myself what I like to call "get lost time." It had been less than a year since the operation and, while I was

Life's Not Over, It Just Looks Different

getting around pretty well on my own most days, there were times when I still got lost or had more difficulty finding a place than I thought I would. Plus, it's part of my personality that I hate being late. I would rather be 20 minutes early than one minute late for anything. Even when I was fully sighted, getting my bearings when I left the subway always took a minute or two. Having less sight meant getting my bearings took even longer, but I got pretty good at knowing which side of the street had odd or even numbered addresses, and that helped a lot. When I reached my desired stop on exam day, I left the subway station and walked a few metres to a major intersection, so I could find out which street I was on. Once I found the street I needed, next I had to find a building with numbers large enough that I could read the address. In fact, I usually liked to find two or more buildings where I could read the address so I could tell which way the numbers were going. I still had about 40 minutes before the exam and knew I was close, so I didn't feel any sense of urgency about finding the building, I just needed to find a number I could read. A little bit of good luck was on my side that day, because the first building I found with numbers large enough to read was the office tower where I needed to be. "That was too easy," I thought. As I walked into the building and started searching for the elevator, I saw a guy who seemed to know where he was going, so I followed him. Once in the elevator, I discovered he was going to the same place to write the exam, as well.

In the exam room, there were a number of people sitting down and others standing, but no one in the room was directing traffic, so I just stood against a wall and waited to see what would happen. I had taken my white cane with me, so they would know I was the one who had requested the special large print copy of the test. After about 10 minutes, one of the administrators came to me and said that I would be sitting in a special cubicle on one side of the exam room, separate from the others. That worked just fine with me. A few minutes later, the exam proctors went around the room placing copies of the exam in front of each student. My copy of the exam was delivered last. The administrator came over to my desk with a stack of 14 by 17 inch paper held together by a large paperclip. There was a loud "thump" as she dropped it on the desk in front of me. The font size was exactly what I had requested; 36-point.

The exam consisted of 100 multiple choice questions and took up about 10 pages. Or at least, that's what the other students received. My large print version had the same 100 questions, but took 52 pages! As part of the accommodation request on the doctor's note, I was given an extra hour to complete the test. I finished the exam with about 10 minutes to spare.

I waited five days for my results. The passing mark was a 60, but I felt pretty good about the exam and was hoping for a score of 80 or better. I came up a little short of my goal and was personally disappointed with the result, but as Cindy and a few friends pointed out, I had passed and that was really all that mattered. With the first exam out of the way, I was free to concentrate on the next textbook and the second exam.

Life's Not Over, It Just Looks Different

ANOTHER PITCH, LOW AND INSIDE

One week after submitting my application for the supervisory position in Calgary, the station's operations manager called to tell me I didn't get the job. He told me which two people they hired, and I couldn't argue with those choices — one of their own staff in Calgary and one of my co-workers from Toronto. Both guys are very smart and deserved the jobs. During the conversation, the manager asked how I was doing; he'd heard I had had a rough autumn. I told him the doctor had recently cleared me to go back to work in some form. He went on to say there were still more jobs to be posted and if I was interested, I should send him an email asking him to refer to my résumé on file.

I called my HR contact in Toronto to tell her what happened, but she was out of the office, so I left her a message asking if she might know why the company policy of interviewing all internal applicants had not been followed.

All of that took place the same day I was to meet with the rehabilitation worker from the insurance company. She asked a number of questions as a follow-up assessment to see if anything had changed since the original claim — questions ranging from work related matters (i.e., how I felt about going back to work) to more personal questions about how I was getting around the apartment and how I kept myself busy during the day. The meeting gave me the opportunity to ask questions about my claim, including getting reconfirmation about what I'd been told about the reoccurrence clause. I asked her if I could work with a career counsellor to start assessing any transferable skills so that I might move on to a life after television. Some of my questions she deferred to the case worker. She told me the insurance company's focus was on getting me back to my job without any real consideration of whether or not the job still existed.

The conversation was frustrating to say the least. I felt she wasn't really grasping the fact that if I returned to my current role in master control, there would eventually be no job and I'd be starting over. I was trying to be proactive for my own career, but the insurance company seemed very short- sighted, only dealing with the issue at hand and not trying to help me move forward.

I showed her a copy of a job posting for a master control position. We went over each requirement and I told her what I could or couldn't do on each point. We had planned to review the posting for the supervisory position as well, but since it had been filled, we didn't talk about it.

The HR person called me back after 4 p.m. that day to tell me she had received my message and had sent an email to her HR counterpart in Calgary. She also copied some of the bosses on the email, asking why the procedure had not been followed. I was sorely disappointed by what had taken place and said flat out that I couldn't help but wonder if I wasn't called because they knew about my sight. She told me not to think that way and said she was hoping to get some response to what went wrong. I wasn't disputing who had been selected for the jobs, I told her. They were both good guys and would do well.

As we were wrapping up our call, there was a call-waiting beep on my phone. It was an upper level manager from Calgary. He said he owed me an apology for what had happened. I told him I couldn't help but feel disappointed by the news and the lack of an interview. He said he understood. He told me it had been his plan to post each of the jobs they planned to hire in Calgary all at once, do the interviews and talk to each person about what they might be interested in, or in some cases, better suited for. He said he still wanted to set up a call with me where he and the operations manager could have a chat with me about other spots they wanted to fill. We set up a time for the following week.

I was glad he called and I liked the idea that I would still get a chance to talk about fitting into the operation in Calgary in some way. Now, perhaps he was just trying to smooth the waters and had no real intention of hiring me, but at the time I was more focused on the prospect of getting to Calgary, showing what I could do in spite of my reduced vision and moving on with my life. I was so tired of being on disability, I think I was just willing to give the entire world the benefit of the doubt.

There were days I got very frustrated at the thought of our department being moved to Calgary. I had applied for jobs in the television business in Calgary off and on over the years, and this should have been my chance to finally get there, but because of my vision loss the job I was most suited for was no longer an option. In my opinion, if it hadn't been for my sight loss, I would've been packing for Calgary instead of sitting and wondering what the insurance company and the workplace were going to come up with as a job solution or at least some assistance to find a new role. All of those conversations that day, the frustration and disappointment that resulted, fueled more anger as my thoughts turned to all the other things I could no longer do with the loss of my sight. My anger and frustration built up to the point where I was nearly in tears.

I hated those days because I wanted to be strong and show the world that I was going to do just fine, but at the same time it was very frustrating to think about how life would have been different if I hadn't lost my sight. I knew my career path and, despite the layoff, I was confident I could have stayed in broadcasting with little or no interruption, but that was all changed by a surgical complication that made the future much more uncertain.

A bomb drops

At the end of March 2006, I had an appointment scheduled with the ophthalmologist to get an assessment of my progress. I'd had a visual field test two months earlier, but had never been told the results. I called the hospital, and the receptionist decided to book me in for another visual field test to make the results more current, so I could see the doctor the same day to talk about the results.

I did the test late in the morning and then waited and waited and waited to see the doctor.

As we sat in the waiting room, Cindy and I could hear a young girl screaming and crying in one of the treatment rooms a short distance away. The fear and agony I sensed from her screams was heart-wrenching and nearly brought me to tears, too.

It turned out my doctor was the one treating the young girl doing all the screaming. When I got to see him, he looked at the test results and said that they weren't really showing him much, because it looked like I had not done the test correctly with one eye. That was annoying; if I'd been doing the test incorrectly, the technician should've said something and started again. Despite this, the doctor carried on, asking me questions about how well I was seeing and what I could see. He did a few quick tests, like having me look at an eye chart and a quick colour blindness test, because I told him I was seeing photographs as negatives. After the tests, he flipped through his paperwork and said he didn't really know what I wanted him to tell me as far as my recovery. He asked how long it had been since the surgery. I told him October.

Then he dropped the bomb....

In his opinion, I had probably reached the end of my recovery.

I was stunned.

I tried to ask him another question, but my nerves were so frayed from listening to the little girl screaming, I couldn't get the words out. I broke down and cried.

Having two patients in a row who were in tears was not a good day for him, either. Although he had trained in neurosurgery, the ophthalmologist told Cindy and I one of the reasons he decided not to become a neurosurgeon was because he didn't like giving people the kind of bad news he had just given me. He tried to soften the blow by telling me I was free to get a second opinion. A second opinion? I had been told he was one of the best in the city. I didn't see much point in getting a second opinion.

I started to regain my composure and told him I wasn't going to seek another opinion and thanked him for his honesty. He flipped through the paperwork some more and said that he didn't know exactly what happened to cause my vision loss, but from what he had in his notes, it had something to do with the blood vessel feeding the occipital lobe of the brain having been cut off from its blood supply. He continued, saying he'd been told the surgeon who operated on me was regarded as the best in the city by his peers and he probably did nothing wrong, but that something had clearly gone wrong to cut the supply of blood to that part of the brain. He told me I could return to his office as often as I wanted to do the visual field test and that he'd sign any papers I needed for disability claims, but that was all he could do for me.

Life's Not Over, It Just Looks Different

Feeling much sadder, but without the tears, we left his office. The rest of that day was a bummer for both Cindy and me. Cindy went to work later that day and told the bosses. I called the HR person and then I called my mom, my sister and my brother to tell them what the doctor said. I needed sympathetic ears on such a lousy day.

THE NEXT MOST COMMON QUESTION I'M ASKED

If the most common question I'm asked is, "What can you see?"; the second most popular question has been, "Did you sue someone for what happened?" I always answer no; I didn't believe the doctor did anything wrong. That was until a follow up visit with the neurosurgeon in February 2006. He made a comment that I was "more shunt-dependent than he thought." At first, his comment didn't really sink in, but after leaving his office it stuck in my head and kept bugging me. It bothered me enough that I thought perhaps I should ask a lawyer about it.

Cindy and I were getting our wills done a few weeks later, and at the meeting I asked the lawyer if she could recommend someone who worked on medical malpractice cases. She gave me two names to call. The first lawyer was out, so I just left a message and called the second lawyer. I told him the story, and he asked me a few questions. He told me it would be a very hard case to fight. The organization that protects doctors from lawsuits fights vigorously to defend doctors and any award that might be won may not be worth the cost to fight the case. For starters, I would have to spend thousands of dollars to get the records and have them reviewed just to see if there was a case. I thanked him for his time and opinion and hung up.

Nearly three weeks passed before I heard from the first lawyer. In fact, his call caught me completely by surprise.

"I was hoping I could bounce something off you," I said

"Only if it doesn't hurt."

"It will only hurt a little."

I told him the story of the first surgery, then the second and while I spoke he didn't say much other than "yup … uh-huh … yup …" until I got to the part about being legally blind.

"Pardon me?" he said.

He admitted he had only been half-heartedly listening up to that point, because he knew a little about shunt surgeries and wasn't really hearing anything out of the ordinary.

He started asking a lot more questions, getting deeper into the story. He said I had definitely called the right person, because he liked to do malpractice cases and, as an added bonus, his father was a semi-retired neurosurgeon, so he was going to run the story by him to see if this was a common risk in these cases. After the call, I told Cindy what he'd said and how his father happened to be a neurosurgeon. Even if I didn't proceed with the case, I felt I might get a few more answers just from the process.

The lawyer called me the next day to tell me he'd spoken to his father and had a few more questions. Without having seen the records, his father said the loss of sight was likely caused by the build-up of fluid around the brain, since it affected both eyes. If it had only affected one eye, then it would be possible that the blood vessel feeding that part of the brain was injured in a mishap of some sort. The lawyer said he would need to request the records and have them reviewed to begin the investigation. We scheduled an appointment for two days later to get the ball rolling.

For me, contacting a lawyer wasn't about suing for money; it was about getting answers to why this happened. In that one phone call, I felt I already had more answers than I had from the hospital or the doctors.

The night before the appointment was not a good one for me. Cindy had gone in late that night to train in a different department. She reassured me she would be home in time to get a bit of sleep before the appointment.

I went to bed rather late, about four in the morning, but woke up about 90 minutes later: Cindy still wasn't home. I tried to fall back to sleep, but all sorts of thoughts started passing through my head. "Was Cindy okay? Had something happened to her?" I began having second thoughts about seeing a lawyer: maybe Cindy wasn't in favour of the idea, either. She told me from the beginning she didn't feel good about calling a lawyer. I began seeing her not coming home from her training as her way of showing disinterest in going to this appointment. As I obsessed about Cindy, my own doubts increased. I wanted answers, but did I want to put out so much money to get them. It could cost as much as $3,000 just to get the records and have them reviewed to see if there was a case at all. And even if there was a case, there was no guarantee that it would go my way. I began to panic at the idea of losing, and got so wound up in my own head, I couldn't sit still. I needed to go for a walk.

First I walked by our workplace to see if Cindy was still there. I found her car in the parking lot, which gave me a pretty good clue she was safe, so at least I could put those thoughts to rest. I didn't go into the building, because I didn't want to tell her what I was feeling in that environment.

I kept walking for a while with a mixed bag of thoughts running through my head. I just didn't want to deal with this anymore. I wished it had never happened. The fear of pursuing a lawsuit and losing was really starting to play on my mind. I started to have ideas of just walking away from everything and getting lost somewhere. But where? How would I get there?

As I walked, I came out of my funk and started to think of the positive things I had going for me. I thought of Cindy and her unwavering love and support. She had stuck by me when others wouldn't. One person even went so far as to tell her she should leave me because I would be a burden on her with less eyesight. Luckily for me, she didn't listen.

When I got back to the condo, I sat on the couch waiting for Cindy to arrive. She walked in about an hour later and looked at me from across the room.

"Hi," she said, as she kicked off her shoes.

"Hi."

"I'm sorry I got home later than I said I would. I got caught up in the training."

"I thought maybe you stayed later because you don't really want to see the lawyer. Do you still want to go?" I asked.

"Oh, I feel awake enough. We can still go to the appointment."

"I've been awake most of the night thinking about it. I'm starting to have second thoughts about talking to the lawyer."

"Why? What's wrong?"

"I'm not sure if this is the right thing to do," I said, choking back tears. "I really want to get more answers, but what if we go to court and we lose?"

I had to stop and catch my breath.

Cindy sat down next to me on the couch and put her hand on my leg.

"If you don't want to go, that's okay. I'll call the lawyer's office and tell them you're not feeling well. That way you can think about it a little longer."

Life's Not Over, It Just Looks Different

I nodded, and whispered, "Okay."

"When do you see the psychiatrist next?" she asked.

"I see him next week."

"Why don't you talk to him before you see the lawyer?"

"Yeah, good idea."

I rubbed my temples with my fingers as I got up from the couch.

"Good. I'll call and cancel. You should try and get some more sleep."

I walked down the hall to our bedroom, while Cindy called the lawyer's office. I lay on the bed with tears still rolling down my face. I had my eyes closed and didn't realize Cindy had come in the room and was watching me, until I opened them after a short time. I felt so bad, I began to cry even harder looking at her and feeling incredibly selfish and stupid.

"Here, this will help with your headache so you can sleep."

She handed me a pain pill and a glass of water to wash it down. I put the empty glass back on my night stand and stretched out on the bed again. Cindy crawled under the covers beside me and shortly after, we both fell asleep.

The following Monday, I had an appointment with the psychiatrist, where I got a chance to tell him what had happened a few days earlier. He didn't seem very comfortable with the idea of me going to a lawyer to pursue some answers and possibly legal action. He said he couldn't tell me what to do either way, but he did ask what I expected to gain by going the legal route. I explained to him that I needed answers. What made that surgery different from the twelve operations before it? I knew about the blood clot and the pressure on my brain, but it wasn't really made clear to me where the pressure came from and, again, hydrocephalus is all about pressure on the brain, so why was it different this time? His response was, sometimes there are no answers other than to say "God knows." He said that sometimes we get to a point where that's the only answer left to the questions we ask.

I wasn't convinced we had reached that point yet. I had this nagging feeling that there were still more answers to be gained from asking the right questions of the right people, and if it took a lawyer to do it, then that would be the way to go.

The appointment with the lawyer was three days later. Before going in, I told Cindy she was going to be the star of the show, because I had no idea what happened in the hospital. If she wasn't comfortable with the idea of going after the information, then we would stop. She was okay with having the records read by another doctor to try to clear up some of the mystery, but beyond that she wasn't sure.

Life's Not Over, It Just Looks Different

In his office, the lawyer would ask Cindy a number of questions and then look at me and ask if I remembered any of it. I told him that, after I threw up in the emergency room, I didn't remember anything except for a small recollection of a chat about the oxygen tube in my nose between the first and second surgeries. He told us he'd had a conversation with a friend of his who was a neurosurgeon. After hearing the story, the friend said that considering what took place, I was lucky to be alive. That was a sobering thought.

Cindy said she had the same feeling as she watched me in the hospital, but didn't really want to tell me that, because she thought it would freak me out. I checked with Cindy again to see if she was comfortable with the lawyer and what he had to say. She was, so we signed the papers for him to request the records and left the office.

A few weeks later the lawyer called to say he had taken a quick glance through the hospital records and saw a few items that suggested there had been delays between the first and second surgery. He was going to try and find out more about those delays. He said he'd need some time to find a doctor who was willing to review the notes and give an opinion, and warned us it could take a few weeks or even months to find a doctor willing to go on the record with an opinion, but that he would follow up with me when he had more information.

JOB SEARCH

Two months after receiving the layoff notice at work, Cindy and I attended a résumé workshop hosted by a counsellor from a firm brought in to assist the staff in our department with moving forward. The layoff was a little over three months away, so we needed to start working on the future. Even though it looked like I wasn't going to be laid off at the same time as my co-workers because I was still on long-term disability, I knew eventually I would need to find a job, so I attended the session looking for any insight the counsellor could offer on what my next steps might look like. During a break in the meeting, I asked the counsellor the same question I had asked others before him: "When was a good time to tell prospective employers about my vision loss?" By this time, roughly six months after the surgery, I was no longer walking with the white cane, so prospective employers wouldn't know until I said something. He said he thought it was a good idea to reveal it early on but not to present it as a problem. Instead, he suggested having a solution for them right after telling them of the issue. He thought it would be a good idea to target employers who would be more accepting of my condition. He said one other thing that I thought was quite smart: "People who ask for jobs get information. People who ask for information get jobs." This really resonated with me and had a big impact on how I approached my job search.

As I reviewed various job postings, I tried to picture myself in those positions. Could I do it? Would I want to do it? Occasionally, I saw a posting that I thought was right for me in many ways except for one or

Life's Not Over, It Just Looks Different

two qualifications listed that I didn't know or didn't have, but if I felt I could do the other things listed and if it seemed interesting, I applied anyway. The way I saw it, as long as I could do most of what they asked, I'd leave it up to the hiring manager to decide if I was right for the job or not. I took the view that "I may not be the best person for the role, but I might be the best they can find."

The second week of May, I had a job interview for a coordinator role in the sales and marketing department at Global. Since the position was quite a departure from my path in broadcasting to that point, when the interviewer looked at my résumé, he naturally asked why I wasn't trying to stay in the operations side of the television business. His question gave me the perfect opportunity to bring my eyesight into the conversation. I told him briefly about my surgery and how I was not going to be able to return to my old position but wanted to stay in the television business and find another way to use my knowledge and experience.

"What do they have you doing at work with your sight the way it is right now?" he asked.

"I'm on long-term disability until they figure out where to put me," I told him. "That's part of why I'm applying for jobs on my own so I can demonstrate what I believe I can do. The insurance company told me if I find a permanent role with another department at the station, they might be willing to pay for the devices I require to do the job."

He paused to think about that for a moment, and then leaned forward slightly to ask, "But what if you had to find a file or some other paperwork away from your desk?"

I pulled my handheld magnifier out from the inside pocket of my suit jacket and held it out in front of me. "I carry this with me everywhere I go and, as long as things are properly filed, I'll do just fine." I smiled as I put the magnifying glass back in the breast pocket of my jacket.

He chuckled knowingly, and I laughed with him, because we both knew that in an office environment, things sometimes get misfiled.

"Well, attitude is everything," he said. "I really must congratulate you for facing the challenge and trying to move forward."

"I am trying very hard not to let this stop me and doing what I can to regain my independence," I said, sitting just a little straighter in my chair. "My goal is to get back to a regular life as much as possible."

We talked about the devices and equipment I felt I needed to do the job, including the CCTV. When I compared it to a microfiche machine as a point of reference for him, he smiled and said he knew exactly what that was because he had previously worked for a company that made and sold that type of equipment. I had such a good feeling walking out of the interview, I knew it was going to be hard to take if I didn't get the job.

Life's Not Over, It Just Looks Different

The red tape thickens

The day after the interview for the sales coordinator role, I called the rehabilitation worker at the insurance company. I told her about the interview and asked how quickly they could provide the tools I needed. I didn't want a delay in getting the devices to cost me the job. She referred me to the CNIB and to the government assistance program. If they could fund a portion of the cost, it would be much easier for her to justify covering the rest.

One week later, I went to the CNIB to discuss CCTV units and whether I was eligible for help with the cost. They showed me two units; one very basic model that displayed in black and white and had no computer connection, the second featuring a colour display that could be hooked up to a computer with a foot pedal to switch between the two units on the same monitor. Of the two units, the latter was not covered by the government program.

Later that day, I called the rehabilitation worker and told her about the two units and the prices I was quoted. She asked about my eligibility for help with the cost of the devices. I was eligible but didn't feel good about using the program, because if my home unit failed, then I was out of luck for help from the program for the next five years. She wasn't sure the insurance company would pay for the devices, because I was not returning to my job but would, in fact, be going to a different job in the company.

"Does that mean the employer would be footing the bill?" I asked.

"I don't think the company will pay for it, either," she said.

"I'm pretty sure that's a human rights issue. If I'm able to do the job, the company has to provide the tools for me to do it," I said.

She wasn't sure about that.

"I find it very hard to believe that every disabled employee ever hired has to provide their own devices to do their jobs!" I was firm, but tried not to let my frustration show. She offered to speak to the HR person at work to find out more.

An end to the red tape

In mid-May, I received an email from the new program manager at VoicePrint. They would have a studio producer spot opening up soon and asked if I would be available for an interview. This was actually the second studio producer job opening in just a few weeks, because the organization was growing. I didn't get the first job, but when the second opportunity opened up, they checked my résumé and called me to come in for an interview.

Life's Not Over, It Just Looks Different

I went in the next morning and sat down with the program manager to talk about the job. The interview only lasted about fifteen or twenty minutes, but I had a good feeling about how it went.

The interview at VoicePrint happened just a few days after the job interview with the sales and marketing department at Global, so now I felt really good because I had two interviews that I thought had gone well and was just waiting for somebody — anybody — to make a decision.

The program manager at VoicePrint called me 11 days later to offer me the job. I asked for a little more money than he'd offered and he had to check with his boss. Ten minutes later, he called back to ask if I could start on the following Monday. I could, indeed.

"Then, we can meet your new salary request," he said.

I was delighted and had to share the happy news. First up — my boss at Global. When I told him, his first question was, "How will that affect your disability payments?" I told him I was calling the insurance company to tell them to keep their disability payment; I would rather work. He said he needed to speak to HR and told me not to leave home until either he or the HR person called me back.

While I waited for that phone call, I called the insurance company to tell the case worker the news. She was happy for me. I made one more call to my original case worker. She was a nice lady and I wanted to share the good news with her, too. She said she wasn't surprised. She knew I wasn't going to stay on disability very long.

Nearly an hour and a half later, the HR person finally called me. She asked about the job and if I had accepted it already.

"Yes, I've already accepted it."

"I called the hiring manager for the sales department to ask if they were close to a decision on the coordinator job and I was told you're the leading candidate," she said. "They're just waiting for one of the executives to finalize the paperwork, but he's out of town right now. Do you want them to call you when the paperwork is ready so you can consider the offer?"

"I don't think that's a good idea. I've already given my word to the manager at VoicePrint."

"Why don't you call the career counsellor and see what he thinks," she suggested.

I reached the career counsellor and told him what had transpired. We discussed how I felt about the job I had accepted and the position that "might" be available to me. We talked for about 45 minutes about both jobs and the situation I was in. More than once in the conversation, he said in his opinion I was doing the right thing. He also told me staying for the sales position was not necessarily a good idea, because he felt the company was in turmoil and if I went there, I might be setting myself up for another layoff down the road.

Talking to the career counsellor made me feel even better about the decision. I called HR back to tell her that I was now even more confident I had made the right decision.

The most disappointing thing about telling the HR person and my boss about my decision that day was that neither one congratulated me for choosing to get on with my life. Seven months after losing my sight, I was going back to work, but they had no kind words for me.

Right from the time I'd started volunteering for VoicePrint 18 months earlier, I knew it was a place that I would like to work someday. I originally thought that time would be much later, when I was no longer having fun in the television business. Losing my sight meant that "someday" came a lot sooner than planned; but not many things in life go as planned.

GETTING BACK TO WORK

Going to work for VoicePrint as my first job back in the working world after being on disability for so long and adjusting to life with less eyesight was a very good experience for me. It allowed me to demonstrate that I was able to work again, and I was in an agency whose mandate was to provide a service for the vision impaired. I had felt the positive energy when I was there as a volunteer. When I became part of the staff, I felt it even more as I worked with the volunteers and my co-workers.

Being one of five vision impaired guys in the office also provided me with an excellent resource to learn how to be vision impaired. If I had questions about how to do something or where to find a device that might help me, the guys were always willing to answer my questions.

My first two days were a little hectic. I was excited, but felt a little overwhelmed with both my new job duties and learning my way around the office.

On the first day, there was a wildcat transit strike that caused a lot of problems for the city of Toronto and especially those who depended on transit for work. Right then and there, I was very glad I hadn't taken the sales and marketing job, because it was downtown. Instead, my commute to work at VoicePrint was a 15-minute walk. Yet another reason I knew I had made the right choice.

Life's Not Over, It Just Looks Different

In the lunch room on my first day, most of the conversation revolved around the transit strike. I was standing with a group of co-workers all asking each other how long it took them to get to work or how each person got to work that day. A couple of my new co-workers asked me, "How did you get in today?"

"I walked."

"You walked?" one of them exclaimed.

"Where did you walk from?"

I smiled and said, "It wasn't far. I only live three blocks from here."

The office was a fun and easy-going place to work. I was not the only vision impaired producer working for the organization. In fact, two of the other studio producers were also vision impaired. On the afternoon of my second day, one of the other producers asked me if I would show him the way to the central equipment room. He took my elbow as I led him to the room, and afterward it occurred to me that we were the embodiment of the old saying. I really was "the blind leading the blind."

On my third shift, I walked into the readers' preparation room to get my first reader of the day, a woman named Kay. As I entered the room, I could see three people, but I had no idea which one she might be so I said, "I'm looking for Kay."

One of the readers, an older gentleman said in a somewhat snarky tone, "There are two men and one woman in this room and you say you're looking for Kay?"

The other readers laughed. In a calm, matter of fact tone I replied, "Well, sir, I'm vision impaired and although I can see three figures in this room, I can't tell who is male and who is female." He quickly apologized for his remark, but I told him not to worry about it. I actually found it funny, but I didn't tell him that.

The reaction I got from the volunteers when I told them about my sight (I revealed it when they tried to point out a word in their articles that they didn't know how to pronounce) was usually one of surprise and some readers said I didn't "look blind." I'm not really sure what that meant, but I took it as a compliment.

Not "looking blind" provided for more funny moments in the first few weeks. Not long after I started there, we had a two-day conference downtown. Prior to the conference, my manager asked me and another co-worker — the token sighted one of the four producers — if we would be willing to help our two co-workers who were completely blind get around at the conference to the washroom, get their lunch, etc. I said I'd be willing to help, but I would have to find these things for myself first and I may need a little help before I could help the others. He said, "Oh that's right. You can't see very well, either!" He told me I got around the office so well, he sometimes forgot.

Life's Not Over, It Just Looks Different

My shift at VoicePrint was 11 a.m. to 7 p.m. each day and, because I lived close by, I volunteered to fill in for the morning producer when he went on vacation. Working early in the morning meant working with a group of readers who didn't know me. I didn't know much about them, either. One morning, I was working with two readers when one asked the other a question about one of the stories he had in his hand. The second reader answered back, "I don't know. Let's ask the sighted producer." This was his less than subtle way of pointing out that I didn't appear to be vision impaired, unlike their usual producer. I shot back, "Who are you calling sighted?"

My job as a studio producer meant recording the volunteers while they did their readings of newspaper and magazine articles. For each session, the volunteers would come in, pick up the material they were scheduled to read and find a place in the readers' prep room to look over their material before going into the studio to record it. When it came time for the volunteers to go into the studio, it was my job not only to test their audio levels before recording, but also to listen along for any garbled or mispronounced words. If I heard something I didn't like, I would stop the reader and either tell them what I heard or ask them about a particular word or sentence that didn't sound right to me. Sometimes, I would stop them because I had heard the subtlest little sound in their throat or in the background of the studio. In the first couple of weeks, I was sometimes a little uneasy about stopping the readers, but it didn't take long for me to gain the confidence to stop for anything I wanted to change. As a result, I gained a reputation for being good at my job and also for being good to work with. Most of the readers knew that if I stopped them in the middle of their read, it was because I wanted the best possible read we could put together.

Since reading news articles from a variety of papers was the organization's reason for being, I became an avid watcher of news programs each day. My primary reason for doing it was to hear how names in the news were being pronounced, so I could help the volunteers do the same. If I heard a name being mispronounced, I would stop the reader, tell them how I had heard it said on television, and we'd carry on from there. Knowing I did this, some readers would approach me before going into the studio to ask about a name or some other words they thought I might know. Sometimes, a reader was surprised I knew a word or a name and would ask how I knew it, to which I would respond: "I know a little bit about a lot of things, but I don't know everything about any one thing."

After working at VoicePrint for two years, I reached a point where I was bored with the day-to-day functions of my job. I still loved working with the volunteers and staff, but I wanted a new challenge. That same year, I had completed the Canadian Securities Course and the Conduct and Practices Handbook Course, so I felt perhaps it was time to look more seriously at what I could do with them.

THE TEA LADY

During one of my visits to the neurosurgeon's office, I asked him if he thought Chinese medicine might be effective in recovering some of my sight. He said he didn't know enough about it to have an opinion and said it wouldn't hurt to try it. Nearly a year after the surgery, Cindy and I visited "the tea lady" our friends had recommended.

She had a small shop in Agincourt, a community in the northeast part of Toronto. From the outside, it was an unassuming little shop in a strip mall. Inside, the walls of the shop were lined with large jars of various herbs, leaves and other things used in different combinations to treat whatever ailed you. The scent in the air was a comingling of many different Chinese herbs. Off to the left was the acupuncture room.

I had mixed feelings about whether or not acupuncture would work for me, but I was curious. The tea on the other hand, I wasn't so sure about, but she said both would work together.

We watched as her assistant packaged up the herbs and things, and then she gave us the instructions. Boil one whole package of herbs each day for 90 minutes and drink one cup before going to bed. The next morning, using the same batch of herbs, boil them again for 30 minutes and drink a half-cup of the brew. Throw out that package and use a new batch the next night.

That night we boiled up the first batch — a very spicy potpourri, not a scent I would use as an air freshener, but not horrible. Then it was time for the true test, the taste. Cindy poured out the first cup and took a sip to experience it for herself and said, "I'm sorry you have to drink this." I laughed and took the cup from her hands to begin my medicine. Yup, it was pretty nasty. The best I could come up with was taking a warm beer and boiling it — I don't even like beer, much less warm beer. But if I was going to try and recover any more sight, I had to give it an honest effort, so — down the hatch! I was given five packages to start with before I was to go back and see the tea lady again and although the taste never got any better, it did get easier to take by day three.

The following Thursday, which was also my birthday, was day one as a pin cushion and round two with a new tea recipe. This was my first time ever having acupuncture and I have to say, it was kind of neat. I didn't know exactly what acupuncture was. I mean, I knew about the tiny needles, but I didn't know how they worked and I had no idea about the electricity.

The Chinese doctor put one needle in each wrist, one in each of my temples, two needles between my eyebrows and one on either side of my face, about a centimetre from each side of my nose. The only ones I really felt going in were the two by the eyebrows, the others were barely noticeable. Once the needles were in, she started talking about the wires.

Wires? What wires??

Life's Not Over, It Just Looks Different

She attached a wire to each needle and said she was going to turn on the electricity so I would feel a small pulse. She started with the ones in my wrists and sure enough, the pulses started, about one per second. Then she started the temples, followed by the ones in the forehead. She asked if I was feeling all of them pulsating.

"Not the ones at the nose," I said.

She gave one of the needles a small twist and turned up the juice a little; ah, now they were working! All of the pulses seemed to be moving at slightly different intervals to one another, which made for a strange, but not a bad feeling.

Once the pulsing started, she told me not to move too much. Well, at some point, that instruction went in one ear and out the other, because after about 10 minutes, I felt the need to reposition my left hand. As I lifted it, I suddenly felt a dull but intense pain in my wrist. It felt like a punch in the arm or a charley horse. I quickly put my hand back where it had been and the pain went away.

After disconnecting the wires and removing the needles, she put some little acupuncture stick-ons at four different spots on each ear. She told me to press them often over the next week.

Before I left, it was time to get the new tea. I tried it that same night. As the tea lady told me at her office, it certainly was different than the last one. I couldn't put my finger on a comparable taste right away either, but it was kind of like a gritty tomato soup texture. Much better tasting than the first one.

At the next visit, she tried to talk me into using a special lotion she was mixing up to put on my eyes. I explained to her that I didn't actually have an eye problem; my vision loss was the result of a brain injury. She said my doctor wasn't telling me the whole story, and co-opted me into trying the lotion, putting it on a cosmetic sponge and then on my eyelids.

As I lay on the table with the sponges on my eyes, my frustration built up. I felt she wasn't listening to me. By the time she came back in the room, I was very wound up and, as she pulled the sponges off my eyes, a single tear rolled down my cheek. She wiped it away without saying anything, but when a second tear rolled down my cheek, she asked what was wrong. I told her I didn't understand how the lotion was going to help. I repeated what I had told her before, that the problem was not with my eyes but with the blood vessels in my brain and I thought she was paying too much attention to my eyes themselves. That's when my frustration really got the best of me and I started to cry. She put her arm around my head and pulled me close to her shoulder. She asked again why I was crying, and I told her it was because I didn't feel like she was listening to me. She said she was just trying to help and to do as much as possible to help me get my sight back.

When I saw her two days later for more acupuncture, Cindy came with me. The doctor told Cindy she thought I was a little nervous, because I

Life's Not Over, It Just Looks Different

wasn't buying into the lotion. She told the doctor if I didn't want to use the lotion, it was my choice.

A few days later, Cindy and I went for a walk and talked about how much I was seeing and if I thought the tea and the acupuncture were working. I had been thinking about it from the start of the treatments, trying to decide for myself if it was working or not. I did notice that my world seemed a little brighter; and the colours I could see, mostly red and yellow, seemed to be more brilliant than before. I wasn't sure if that was improvement from the tea and the acupuncture or just time. I didn't seem to be reading any smaller fonts, so I wasn't sure if my sight was still improving. Cindy said she was going to start testing me again as we had done months earlier with different font sizes.

The following week, she did just that. We started at 26-point font and moved down by twos. I was able to read down to the 14-point font. This didn't mean I would be able to read an entire document in that, but it was a step above the last time we had checked, when I was only able to make out 16-point font.

By the time I was on to my fourth tea recipe, I was starting to feel encouraged by small signs of progress. Aside from the brighter colours, one of the first things I felt I was seeing better were people's features. I was starting to notice details about people I either hadn't seen in a while or, in the case of the volunteers I worked with at VoicePrint, details I'd never seen.

After a couple of weeks with the tea, I started to notice people's hairstyles more, as well as the shade of their hair. I still couldn't really tell exact colours, but I was starting to notice the difference between blondes and brunettes. One day, I was telling one of the volunteers about the changes I was starting to see, and as we spoke, it dawned on me that he was balding from the centre of his forehead to the crown of his head. Cindy, and the acupuncturist were pleased. The acupuncturist, in particular, saw it as validation that her treatment was working.

These changes made me feel good about what was happening, and Cindy and I both thought it was a good idea to continue, as long as there was some tangible progress being made. But at the same time, I had lingering doubts about the doctor. Her belief that it was an eye problem and not a brain injury as the hospital tests had shown still bothered me. Early in the treatment, I started to see colours a little brighter and some other changes, but nothing really changed since those first few days.

The last weekend in October, the Chinese doctor told me she was going away for three weeks and I should stock up on the tea. I wasn't keen on that, and she did exert a subtle pressure for me to continue, but I didn't give in. It just wasn't sitting right.

I did see another acupuncturist in 2007, but only for two months. This one, a Korean doctor, did diagnose me accurately as having a brain injury, but, ultimately, I wasn't convinced the treatments were doing much. The cost was also weighing on my mind. None of this was covered by my health insurance.

I'm not sure how much of the improvement I saw could be attributed to the treatments or if my body was still healing itself. Even then, was it the tea? Perhaps it was the acupuncture? I have no idea. In the end though, I had tried both things and was okay with the decision to stop.

TEST DAY

Saturday March 31, 2007, was a day of tests for my abilities and my knowledge.

The first order of business for the day was my last exam for the Canadian Securities Course. Saturday was the absolute last day I could take the exam, since that was when my year ran out. Why did I do it on the last possible day? Because the exam was only held one Saturday a month and this was it.

The location for the exam had moved since I'd taken the first exam six months earlier, so I had to find the new location. I searched out an online map, and it looked like the location was going to be pretty easy to access from the subway line. Just to be sure, I left 90 minutes before the exam as per my "get lost time" rule.

I took my white cane with me, because I wanted them to know I was the vision impaired guy writing the test that day. I felt a little silly about it since I had stopped using it months earlier and, in fact, the previous exam date was probably the last time I had taken the cane anywhere.

Once on the subway line, I couldn't remember the name of the station I needed (it was on a part of the line I didn't travel very often), but I knew it was one stop past Union station on the University line, so I took the long way around, using the Yonge Street train. When I got to my station (St. Andrew), I followed the signs out to King Street and started to walk west, hoping it wasn't going to be far. It had looked like a short walk on the online map and, surprisingly, it was even shorter than I expected. I found the cross street I needed and started looking for numbers on any of the buildings to give me a point of reference.

The CNIB mobility worker had suggested establishing my own landmarks, which proved very useful. Over time, I taught myself a few other things that really helped me find my way around the city. One of the first of these was following the sun. It sounds old-fashioned, I know, but it works. If I'm trying to figure if I need to go east or west, I follow the sun. I also got a tip from a Toronto bus driver: odd numbered addresses are on the south side of east-west streets and on the east side of north-south streets.

The day of the exam, I couldn't find any numbers on the first few buildings that were easily readable for me, but I saw a building a short distance ahead that seemed to be the only one on the block tall enough to have a 15th floor. Sure enough, it was the place I wanted. When your sight isn't as good as it needs to be, logic becomes a very valuable tool.

Prior to the exam, I had been told I would be given three hours for the test, instead of the usual two, and that I could write the exam in an empty office with a proctor to assist me. When I arrived, I was shown to a seat in the classroom with everyone else, at a table with one other person. Once the test began, I found myself wishing I had been put in a room of my own. The person next to me murmured the questions to himself as he did the test, which I found distracting. To top it off, he started to sweat and I soon noticed he smelled, too!

The exam was 100 multiple choice questions — under normal circumstances about ten or fifteen pages in regular print. But as you know from reading thus far, I'm not normal. Similar to the first test, it was printed on 14 by 17 inch paper, but this time I'd requested the font size be reduced from a 36 to a 28-point font. It still took up 62 pages!

The exam supervisor announced there were only ten minutes left. When she walked over to me, I said, "I was told I would have three hours."

She turned to the front page of my exam and saw it said three hours on it. She apologized and walked back to her desk. I finished the exam with about 15 minutes to spare.

Afterwards, I was feeling pretty pumped up, mostly because the exam was over, but also because I was off to my next test that day, this time at the go-kart track! I had been eager to try running a few laps for some time, just to see what I could do. I wasn't looking to get into a race, just laps. I felt I had recovered enough sight by then that I could run my laps safely. After the exam, Cindy and I got together with our friends, Matt and Renée. Matt had never been in a racing kart before and was eager to try it. Cindy and Renée preferred to watch from the safety of the upper viewing area. Cindy was a little concerned because she didn't want to see me get hurt, but I was pretty sure I could do it with no problem. Matt and I paid for our laps and proceeded to the track, where we hopped into a couple of karts. This was my first time in a go-kart since the change in my sight, so I understood why Cindy was nervous. But people can't see through my eyes, so they don't know what I can and can't see.

I went out first; Matt followed, and four others came out on the track behind us. I drove the first lap at a moderate speed. The track had been partly redesigned since I had last been there, and I wanted to get a feel for the changes. Road racing requires a certain amount of memory work so that a driver will know how to approach each corner of the track. The track wasn't much different than it had been before my vision was reduced and, by the time I came around for the second lap, I had a pretty good understanding of the layout. I floored the accelerator for the long straightaway and it felt great!

Since I went out first, I had nothing but empty track in front of me for about the first ten laps. None of the people behind me had caught up to pass me and I didn't realize Matt had dropped back in the group until I found out he was the first kart I was about to lap. He looked back, saw me behind him and pulled over for me to pass. He told me later he was "letting me by" but he also admitted it wasn't going to be long before I passed him anyway. A few laps later, I came up behind one of the people I didn't know. He didn't let me pass as easily as Matt had, but he didn't fight me, either. The third person I passed was someone who had spun out on the track. He was being pushed back from the tire barrier when I came upon him.

We were set to run 20 laps in total that day. I wasn't sure how many we had completed at that point, but I started to wonder if I was going to be able to see the track worker signalling for us to pull in to the pits. As I ran the next few laps, I started looking toward the pit entrance as I went by, looking for any sign of a track worker calling me in. I didn't see anyone by the entrance, but I decided I had been out there long enough and pulled in to the pits. A track worker came up and asked if I had been counting my own laps — I had gone exactly twenty. When we finished, I went to the counter to get my lap times. Another track worker handed them to me, but not wanting to let on that I couldn't read the sheet, I put it in my pocket to read later.

All in all, I thought it was a successful test. My fastest lap was 35.15 seconds, which was about one second off the fastest lap of the day. It dawned on me later that I was about as fast as I had been before losing my sight, which told me one of two things: either I was really fast with limited eyesight or really slow as a fully sighted person! Cindy told me later that her concerns about me being out there went away as she and Renée watched me circle time after time.

With both of the day's tests complete, I was feeling really good. I would have a few days to wait until I got the results of the exam, but I was fairly confident I'd passed. As for the laps on the go-kart track, I knew I still wasn't going to be driving a car anymore, but I could still enjoy one of my favourite hobbies now and then.

Life's Not Over, It Just Looks Different

STILL LOOKING FOR ANSWERS

In early September 2007, the lawyer called. He said he was having trouble finding an expert to look over the medical records and give an opinion, but he was still trying. He went on to tell me that the two-year statute of limitations was drawing near and he wanted to know if we were still interested in pursuing the matter. If we were, he said, we'd have to file a notice of statement of claim in order to buy a little more time while he continued to look for an expert. I told him I needed time to think about it. Cindy still wasn't really on side with the idea of the lawsuit, although she understood my need for answers.

I decided to ask someone I knew who had a legal background for some advice. Filing a notice was not a bad idea to buy more time, she told me, but she also advised calling the hospital's patient advocate office again until I got some answers.

I called the patient advocate's office for about three weeks straight, each time getting an answering machine saying she was on vacation, but she finally did call me back. I gave her a brief rundown of what had happened to me and told her I had tried to talk to someone in her office on a few occasions earlier to no avail. She expressed shock and apologized, saying there had been some turnover in her department. When I told her the lack of response from her department caused me to go another route and find a lawyer, she replied, "Good!" Getting a lawyer was not my first choice, I told her. I really just wanted answers, not a lawsuit. She suggested talking to the doctor directly, telling him that even after all this time, I wasn't comfortable with what had happened.

In our conversation she asked how I was doing at that time — was I working, and how was my wife handling the situation?

I was able to answer her questions without hesitation until she asked about Cindy

"She's been amazing," I said, barely able to get the words out. I choked up and had to catch my breath before I could say another word. She waited patiently while I collected myself and then repeated what she wanted me to do and asked me to call her back the next week to let her know what happened.

In early October, I was still mulling over the idea of whether or not to proceed with the lawsuit. At the same time, work was really busy and both things were stressing me out. Cindy and I talked about it and I also bounced my thoughts off the psychiatrist. He helped me with the work stress, but said he couldn't take a position on what to do about the possible legal action.

I decided not to go ahead with any legal proceedings. My lawyer told me it was a shame; he thought I had a pretty good basis for a legal case. I still had questions, but didn't feel good about trying to get those answers through the courts. He told me if I changed my mind later the door would be closed once the statute of limitations ran out at the end of October. I was okay with that.

Life's Not Over, It Just Looks Different

The next thing I did was call the neurosurgeon's former secretary to get a message to him because I still had questions. He had retired but I figured she would know how to get in touch with him. She found out he was going on vacation but she would pass on the message. I then called the patient advocate and told her about the request. She called me back a few days later and said, if I didn't get a call back from the doctor, she would try to talk to the head of Neurosurgery on my behalf.

Two weeks later, I had another appointment with the psychiatrist and told him my work stress had been reduced and that I had decided not to proceed with legal action. He made no comment. We discussed the questions that still weighed on my mind, and he said he was sure no one had done anything with malicious intent. I didn't think anyone had either, but I had learned from the lawyer that there were some notes in the medical records that didn't look right.

When I told the psychiatrist what was in the records, he stopped and looked at me for about two minutes without saying anything. Then he asked how I would know if I was having shunt trouble and if a headache was the first clue. I told him yes and that the 2005 headache had seemed more intense than the headache in 2001. He didn't say anything else and instead just looked at me for about ten more minutes.

It was a really odd feeling. He just stared without saying a word. I could tell from his body language that he was thinking something. I waited for him to ask another question or share his thoughts, but he just kept staring. After the prolonged silence, he looked at his watch and said we should stop there for the day. I walked out of his office thinking his reaction was strange, but I had no idea what was behind it.

A couple of weeks after leaving a message for the neurosurgeon he called me back. We played telephone tag until I told his receptionist I needed to speak to him in person.

He called again, and this time he left a message saying if I could be at the hospital the next morning at 8:30, he would meet me there. I called the receptionist back and told her I would absolutely be there the next morning.

Later that same day, I was speaking to a friend who happened to be a lawyer. I told her about the meeting and the list of questions I had for him. She advised me to try not to be adversarial in my line of questioning. She suggested I phrase my questions in a way that was more leading and open- ended, and then to just listen. She felt I would likely get more information out of him than if I went in looking for a fight. I went home and revised my questions, trying to phrase them in a way that didn't speak directly to what I had read in the medical records.

The next day, I arrived at Sunnybrook at 8:15 a.m. and waited outside the office. The doctor came down the hall a few minutes later and invited me in. I said even though it'd been two years since the surgery I still had questions.

Life's Not Over, It Just Looks Different

I started off asking the most obvious question; how did this happen? His response was a very technical one that I couldn't recite if I tried, but basically the fluid had built up in an unusual place in the back of the brain and put pressure on the blood vessels in that area. He said what had occurred was so unusual he couldn't find any evidence of it ever happening before in any of the medical literature he checked. I asked if he was going to write it up, so there would be a record of it for future surgeons. He said he was considering it. In my original list of questions, there were three things that bothered me: One of the pages in the records said, "Do CT now" in big letters. When I was considering a lawsuit, this was the one page that caught the lawyer's attention as something he felt needed a response from the doctor or the hospital. The records showed a CT of my head was called for in the morning but not done until after that note was written. I wanted to ask if the delay in doing the CT contributed to my sight loss.

According to the notes, about an hour after the CT was done, the doctor was called and apparently told I would need further surgery. The response written in the notes said, "We can wait until morning." That was at 6 p.m. Two and a half hours later it was decided I couldn't wait. The surgery started nearly three hours after that, at 11 p.m. I wanted to ask about the timeline and why it took more than five hours to get me in for the second operation. In a roundabout way, I think I got an answer to that question, because he told me since he had semi-retired, he was no longer getting called at all hours of the day for surgeries. Plus, I started putting it together in my own head. If he said at 6 p.m. that I could wait, that's his call. If he's told at 8:30 p.m. that I can no longer wait, it may have taken him an hour or more to get to the hospital to do the surgery. Perhaps there was no operating room or surgical team available.

In his office, I didn't want to let on that I had a copy of the records. I tried to revise my questions so I might still get answers to the three questions without asking directly and possibly getting his back up and having him end the conversation. One thing I was curious about was the CT scan that was requested after the first surgery. There was a note saying to do the CT scan and then later that day there was another note saying, "Do CT Now!!" suggesting it hadn't been done yet. I asked if doing a CT after surgery to see if everything was running smoothly was normal practice, hoping he would tell me about the delay in getting the CT done. He didn't. In fact, he told me the opposite. Doing a CT was not normal course. I asked that question later in the conversation in another way, but got the same answer.

During the one-on-one with the doctor I did get answers to other questions, like what kind of shunt I had in my head. I attended a seminar months earlier talking about all the different models of shunts and came to the conclusion I had no idea what kind I had. At the seminar, they taught us that using the correct shunt is a balancing act for the doctor and patient to drain the right amount of fluid. Drain too little or too slowly, and the pressure on the brain causes headaches. Drain too much too fast and it can cause headaches from a shortage of fluid. The shunts I've been provided with over the years seemed to drain just the right amount because I have only suffered headaches

Life's Not Over, It Just Looks Different

when the shunt was blocked or damaged. That day in the doctor's office I learned I had a medium flow shunt. He told me surgeons typically have certain models they favour, and the medium flow was his first choice.

Another concern I was able to ask about was if I was now at risk for further complications of this type, or if my blood vessels have weakened and might be vulnerable to further damage when it's time for the next revision. He said that was unlikely, but because we learned I was very shunt-dependent, I should come to the hospital at the first sign of trouble. I told him I always try to make sure I'm actually feeling a shunt headache and not a sinus headache, but I also related a prior experience at the same hospital back in 2001 when I was in for a shunt revision. When I told the neurosurgical resident I thought I was having a shunt failure, she asked how I could be sure it was a shunt problem, in a tone that suggested I was in no position to diagnose myself. The surgeon apologized for that. He said they usually have really good residents in their system, but occasionally there's one who isn't.

I asked if it would be better to go to another hospital for my next shunt revision because Sunnybrook is a very busy place. He said that wasn't necessary, because he would feel very comfortable with any of his colleagues performing my future surgeries. He also said if I received any resistance from the emergency ward or a resident, to have them call him and he would speak for me. In my opinion, that right there was a good reason not to have gone in spoiling for a fight and pointing fingers.

My final question was why Cindy had been the one to discover my sight problem instead of one of the doctors or nurses. He asked how she found the problem and I related the experience with the dinner tray when the nurses asked her to see if she could get me to eat. He said that unfortunately the nurses are sometimes in a rush when they drop off the food tray and move on without waiting to see if the patient eats or not. I also asked if he or the resident would've done the "follow my finger" test and, if so, wouldn't the vision loss have been detected then? He said patients who experience cortical blindness sometimes don't realize it right away, or will say they see things when they really don't. He said he had experienced cases of cortical blindness where he suspected something was wrong and confirmed it by asking the patient to look out the window and describe what they saw. When the patient describes something different than what is out the window, that's when the blindness is revealed.

I wrapped up our conversation after about 90 minutes and thanked him for his time. I got some answers that I didn't have prior to meeting with him but, after leaving his office, I had second thoughts about the questions I didn't ask. When I didn't get the answer I had hoped to hear about the delay with the CT scan, perhaps I should have changed gears and asked more pointed questions. Maybe I should have told him I had the notes and asked more direct questions about things I'd read. In reality, though, that day in his office was two years past the surgery and my sight had basically levelled off. Trying to pick a fight looking for answers wasn't going to bring my sight back.

Life's Not Over, It Just Looks Different

ADVENTURES IN TRAVELLING

In mid February 2006, Cindy and I went to Ottawa for a few days to visit her aunt and uncle and to take in a concert by my favourite country performer, Lisa Brokop. February in Ottawa is also the time for Ottawa's annual winter festival, so while we were there I took the chance to skate on the Rideau canal, something I'd wanted to do for many years. I skated with a friend of Cindy's aunt and uncle who kept an eye on me as we went down the ice. We skated a kilometre or two and I only fell three times, so I was pleased with myself, especially since I hadn't been on skates in a long time. Eventually my guide, who was a much better skater than me, said, "We can keep going as far as you'd like. Just remember we have to skate back." Good point, I thought. We skated a little longer, but then turned back to where the others were waiting for us.

In late August 2006, I took on a new challenge — travelling to another city on my own. I went to my cousin's wedding in northwestern Ontario. To make the trip a little easier for myself and so that the airlines would know that I may need some assistance, I took my identification cane with me. At the security check, I put my bags on the conveyor belt to be scanned, and the gate officer asked to scan my cane. I found that amusing, but handed it over. Needless to say, the cane and I both made it through the security check without setting off the alarms. At the Winnipeg airport my luggage passed by me three times before I finally identified it by a broken wheel. Once I confirmed the bag was mine by reading the address label with my magnifier, I found my way to the gate for my connecting flight to Red Lake. The 45-minute flight from Winnipeg to Red Lake was an adventure all its own. It was in a small plane that also had an open doorway to the cockpit. From where I sat, I could see the pilot wrestling with the controls as he resisted the force of the winds. There were times it looked more like he was wrestling an alligator than flying a plane!

This trip was the first time some of my family members would see me since I'd lost my sight, so this was my chance to let them see how much I could do and how I got around. The weekend started out like most other meetings with friends who were seeing me for the first time in that they were trying to guide me places, telling me to watch out for things they weren't sure I could see and most importantly, telling me to watch out for the kids so that I didn't step on any of my nieces.

At the wedding, I was to be the co-emcee. One of my tasks was to read the list of out of town guests that had been printed off for me in 36-point font. I didn't let on to the crowd about my lack of sight until I mispronounced one of the names on the list of guests and was corrected by many members of the crowd. At that point, I showed my list to the audience and said, "You know you're in trouble when they print it off this big and you still mess it up!"

Nearly a year later, I flew to Winnipeg again, this time for a surprise retirement party for one of our former broadcast teachers, a man I call Mr. P., because even as an adult, I still cannot bring myself to call him by his first name.

Life's Not Over, It Just Looks Different

This trip was only my second flight on my own. For the most part, it all went smoothly. I checked in on my own using one of the new check-in kiosks installed at the airport and my magnifier. I made it all the way to my seat on the plane without assistance, and only a minor issue at security, when the security officer found all my "blind toys" (magnifier, monocular and white cane) in my hip pack, which showed up as unusual objects.

I took a taxi to the retirement party because I wasn't familiar with the bus connections in that part of Winnipeg. It was the first time I had seen anyone from the school since 2005. They were a little surprised to see me get around so easily with reduced sight. At the bar, a female voice called out, "Is that Mick Gordon?" Well, there are only four people on the planet who ever call me Mick and only three of them knew me as Gordon, so even though I couldn't recognize their faces, I knew the voices belonged to former co-workers of mine who had attended the same school a few years before I did. Mingling isn't easy when you can't recognize the faces of anyone in the room.

The guest of honour arrived about 40 minutes after I did. One of the teachers later told me he teared up when he heard I'd travelled so far to come to his retirement party.

He had a lot of schmoozing to do that night, but eventually he found me and said, "Ok, tell me you didn't come to town just for this."

"Of course I did," I replied and he choked up again.

"I'm floored you made the trip just to see me!" I tried to downplay it and said it wasn't that big of a deal. I was not the only person who had come in from out of town. Mr. P. played a role in launching the career of many broadcast students, including mine, so I felt it was important to be there to celebrate his retirement.

Finding My Own Way

All forms of mass transportation or public transit became very important once I was no longer able to drive. Cindy still had the car and drove many places, but there were times when she wasn't available, so other modes of transportation came into play.

One of my favourite things is auto racing and go-kart racing is a clear favourite. I frequented the handful of go-kart tracks in and around Toronto between 2001 and 2005. Most were in parts of the city that didn't have convenient transit service, and one place I really liked was in Brampton, just northwest of Toronto, about 50 kilometres from our home.

The tracks weren't easy to get to on my own, and Cindy doesn't enjoy racing as much as I do, so I found myself with a bit of a dilemma. I didn't want to impose on my friends and wanted even less to feel like a child asking to be "taken" to the track. It was frustrating not to be able to take part in one of my favourite activities as often as I'd like.

Life's Not Over, It Just Looks Different

In June 2008, I got tired of waiting for someone to take me racing and decided it was time to get there on my own. I looked up the Brampton kart track on the Internet and found out there was a commuter bus service that had a station near the facility. Actually, on the map it looked like it might be a one-hour walk from the station to the track, but I was willing to do it. There were other tracks closer to home, but Brampton was my favourite.

So, one day as Cindy slept after her midnight shift, I took the bus and subway down to the commuter bus terminal in downtown Toronto and boarded the bus to Brampton. We arrived at the Brampton bus terminal about 30 minutes later. I wasn't sure which way to walk from there, because I hadn't figured out if the terminal was on the north or south side of the street I needed to follow. All I knew was that I needed to walk west of the bus station. I tried using the sun as a reference point, but it was mid-day and directly overhead, which made determining east or west difficult, so I just picked a direction and started walking. Without either a smart phone, GPS or a printed map, I had to rely on my general knowledge of the area and my gut feeling to get me there. After about 40 minutes, I determined that I was walking the wrong way, so I turned back and walked the other way. About a half an hour later, I knew I was headed the right direction based on what I remembered from the map on the Internet, and that was half the battle.

By this time, I had been walking for over two hours, and it was hot outside. I came across a familiar store that I knew was close to my destination and stopped inside for a cold drink and the key to their public washroom.

Eventually, I got tired of looking for the place and making wrong turns, so I called directory assistance from my cell phone and got the number for the go-kart track. I got directions to the track, which wasn't much further, and resumed walking with a new sense of enthusiasm and determination. I was really close now and excited to get there to do some racing!

Once I got there, I had a lot less time to spend on the track; they had a private group taking over the place at 4 p.m. that afternoon and I arrived at the track at 3:20 p.m. I paid for my laps and went down to the staging area. Two other guys were going out on the track at the same time and had the karts in front of me.

As we started rolling, it didn't take me long to pass the first guy when he lost control and spun in a turn. His friend however, was a little tougher. For the first few laps after clearing the first guy, I couldn't even see the second guy because he was so far ahead. But I drove as hard as I could and eventually got right up behind him. Once he realized I was there, he began to race too hard, not running very smooth laps, so I stayed behind him until he made a mistake. I passed him cleanly, but he wasn't far behind: now he had a reason to chase. With about three laps to go in our session, I made an error, going a little wide in one corner, and he was able to pass me back. From there, I was able to stay on his tail, but couldn't pass him before our session ended. A few minutes later, the private group came in, so that was it for racing that day.

It had taken me five and a half hours to get to the track to do 12 minutes of racing before leaving for another four and a half hour journey home. Was it worth it? Absolutely! The best part of making the trip was the feeling of accomplishment I had at having done it on my own.

A TOAST TO A NEW ADVENTURE

There have been surveys done over the years suggesting that the fear of public speaking ranks highest on the list of most people's biggest fears. Apparently, it ranks higher than a fear of spiders, heights, or even the fear of being mauled by a bear. If those survey results are true, then I must be crazy, because I love public speaking!

I first learned about Toastmasters when I was in my early twenties. It stayed with me over the years and, in 2008, I finally decided to look into it further. I found a club that met in a church not far from where I lived. Tom, the club's president that year, was the first to greet me when I visited the club for the first time. I liked the vibe I got from the group and signed up on my third visit.

One of the goals for people in the Toastmasters program is to give a speech without using any notes. When I joined the club, it had been a little over two years since the surgery and, by then, I had a pretty good idea that trying to read out loud from notes in front of people was not going to work very well for me, so I knew I would have to memorize as many of my speeches as possible. Right from the first speech I gave in front of the club members, I didn't use notes.

When I first joined, I told myself I didn't want to make too many speeches about my eyesight. I heard some of the members talking about speakers they had met over the years who only seemed to talk about one core subject and wrote each of their speeches around that

Life's Not Over, It Just Looks Different

topic. I didn't want to be that guy. That's not to say I never used stories of my recovery or experiences in speeches, but I tried to vary it, or use it in creative ways. One of the first speeches where I did talk about it was a short piece about each of the five senses and what I liked, or didn't like about having each one. Things like:

Hearing: I love music, so not being able to hear my favourite song ever again would be devastating to me. On the upside, not being able to hear would mean not being subjected to the sound of someone scratching fingernails on a chalkboard.

Taste: I would miss not being able to enjoy my favourite foods, like lasagna or pizza. On the other hand, if I couldn't taste foods properly, I might not dislike beets or peaches as much as I do.

Smell: If I didn't have my sense of smell, I wouldn't have to worry about running into a skunk. Others around me might be really bothered if I ran into one, but I wouldn't have to care. Though, I would miss the smell of freshly-cut grass or bread baking in the oven.

Touch: Without the sense of touch, a person in business could have difficulties when meeting with clients. He might misjudge the pressure to apply to a handshake and either come off as uncommitted to it, or squeeze the living daylights out of the other person's hand! But the upside to losing the sense of touch — when you go the doctor or the blood donor clinic, needles wouldn't hurt!

And finally, there's sight: Sight allows you to see a beautiful sunrise or sunset, the smile of a loved one, or the reaction of someone who is listening to what you're saying. Like anything else though, there are upsides to not having your sight. You'd never see a man trying to look good in a Speedo.

Doing that speech was actually therapeutic for me in some ways. It made me value the abilities I still had and also made me realize that losing my sight was not the worst thing for me. I determined that of the five senses, I'd miss my hearing the most.

My first few speeches were all written from a humorous point of view whenever possible. Each speech had learning objectives I had to meet, but the content was up to me, and making people laugh or smile is always fun, so I wrote my speeches that way too. One day, a member of the club mentioned that she'd like to see me try something a little more serious. I decided to tell the story of my first walk out of the apartment on my own, in the dark, and I told it basically the way it was written earlier in this book.

As I told the story, I acted out parts of it, moved around the room to make eye contact with the audience and when I got to the part where I told them about making it back home after being so scared and breaking into tears when I called Cindy, I had to catch my breath as a single tear rolled down my cheek during the speech.

Life's Not Over, It Just Looks Different

When I was done, there was a sombre tone in the room and the emcee seemed unsure what to say next as he thanked me for the speech. At the end of the meeting some members came to talk with me.

"You actually cried during your speech! You were right in it, weren't you?" the first one said.

The club member who had suggested I do something more serious said, "That was a really hard story to tell, wasn't it?"

I smiled and said, "You said you wanted to see me do something more serious."

There were times when using notes was almost unavoidable. Sometimes, instead of being the one to give a speech, I was tasked with being a speech evaluator, providing verbal feedback to one of the evening's speakers. In those cases, I had to take notes as I watched someone else speak and then present an evaluation in front of the group. This was a two-part problem for me. The first was being up in front of the group and having to use notes, which I was never comfortable with. The second problem was reading my own writing. My handwriting has become atrocious since losing my sight and if I try to write too quickly, it's unreadable for anyone, not just me. To counter this, I often wrote my evaluation notes in just a few words to prompt myself and then ad-libbed the rest. It worked most of the time, but when it didn't, I felt really embarrassed being up there unable to read my own notes. On the few occasions that I wasn't able to read my writing, or that I had trouble reading it while up in front of the audience, I tried my best to remain calm in front of the group and made jokes about not being able to read my own writing. Inside though, I wanted to be anywhere else at that moment. Luckily, Toastmasters members as a whole tend to be very supportive people, so no one ever said anything to me about it.

During the four years I was part of Toastmasters, I had a great time. I challenged myself to take on different roles in the club, but I also knew which roles were going to be beyond me. Most didn't involve reading out loud, except the role of Toastmaster itself. Each night, it was the Toastmaster who gave the toast for the evening and then conducted the formal speaking session, which included reading out speech introductions provided by each of the speakers. Again with the support of my fellow club members, I was able to arrange that I was never assigned that role at the meetings, so I wouldn't have to read out loud in front of the group.

Being in Toastmasters was a great experience. I met some fabulous people, not only in our own club, but also in other clubs around the city. Most of all, being in Toastmasters gave me a huge amount of confidence and taught me how to control my nervousness when speaking in front of people. I like to joke that I'm not afraid to be in front of people because I can't see their faces well enough anyway and you can't be afraid of what you can't see!

Life's Not Over, It Just Looks Different

A COMPLETE CAREER CHANGE

When I enrolled in the Canadian Securities Course, I didn't know whether I would use it professionally or not. At that time, all I knew for sure was that I was bored sitting at home recovering and had a pretty good idea I wasn't going to be able to return to my old job.

After completing the CSC in March 2007, I was glad that it was over. But two months later, I found myself looking for something else to study. On a website that listed financial industry careers and the courses needed to work in each role, I found out the Conduct and Practices Handbook course (CPH) was a requirement for a handful of different roles, so I decided to take that next.

I completed the exam for the CPH in late January 2008. Unlike the two CSC exams, for the CPH exam I was shown to a meeting room where I wrote the test alone with only a proctor. For all the financial industry exams, I was allowed 50 per cent more time to finish the test due to my condition. It was a good thing, too, because I used nearly the entire three hours to complete the test.

With the CSC and CPH courses under my belt, I began to think more seriously about entering the financial industry, but I wasn't sure what to do next. Do I take more courses? Do I try to find a job? I wasn't sure what my next step should be, and then the advice I had received from the career counsellor brought in by Global came to mind: "People who ask for jobs get information. People who ask for information get jobs." I emailed three people I knew who worked in different parts of the financial industry and two others whose names I'd been given by friends. I told them about the courses I had taken and asked for their advice on where to go next. Did I have enough education to get started in the business? Should I study more before trying to find a job?

I received responses from all five. A couple of them met with me in person and some I spoke to by phone. All of them offered great advice and encouragement. One asked for my résumé and said she'd pass it on to some people at the bank where she worked.

Within a couple of weeks, I received emails to set up meetings with others at the bank. The first two meetings were basically get-to-know-you sessions so they could find out where I wanted to go in the business and where to start. Since I was new to the business, they said I should begin in the bank and work my way up. I agreed and we set up an interview for me to meet with a human resources officer.

Although I wasn't using the white cane anymore, the HR person knew about my sight. When she came to the reception area to greet me, she began leading me down the hall, but then stopped, stepped aside and said, "It's the third door on your right." As I made my way to the office, she followed behind me. I felt like it was a test to see just how much I could see or for her to determine if I was really vision impaired at all. We had a brief interview, during which I learned all she had was a sales job. Within a few days, she wrote to say she had nothing for a person with my skills.

Life's Not Over, It Just Looks Different

Undaunted, I decided to enroll in another course while I kept testing the waters and applying to various roles in financial services. The next course I tackled was the Professional Financial Planning Course (PFPC). I thought financial planning was a good path for me, because it covered many different aspects of personal finance, including budgets, insurance, investments and taxes.

A few months after the interview at the bank, a friend told me about a presentation he had attended where they were recruiting people for jobs with an investment company. He said it wasn't what he wanted to do, but he thought I might like it and told me they were having another presentation very soon. He gave me the contact person's phone number and I reserved a spot at the next presentation.

The presentation was held in the boardroom of the firm's downtown Toronto location. It was hosted by the branch manager of that office and one of his team leaders. They told the group about the role and the income potential ahead for those who stepped up to take the job. They invited anyone who was interested to set up a first interview to learn more.

The position was primarily a commission sales role. There was some residual income that would come along once the person built a list of clients, but initially it was all about drumming up business. I wasn't too sure about taking on a commission sales role, but I was intrigued enough to at least go through the first interview.

During the interview, I was honest with the team leader and his assistant about my eyesight. They didn't seem bothered by it. I brought it up in a positive way, telling them it was a challenge I had overcome and not only was I working again, I had also completed the two investment courses despite my low vision and was working on a third.

After successfully completing the three-interview process, I was offered a job as a financial consultant with the company. Two weeks later, in October 2008, I left VoicePrint to take my first job in financial services.

It was hard to leave the staff and volunteers at VoicePrint. They were a fun group to work with and had made my two and a half years there a memorable experience. The job itself, however, wasn't challenging me enough anymore, so it was time to take on a new adventure.

During the first week at the investment firm, I was introduced to a consultant in the office who I was told was going to be my field trainer. His role, once I finished the classroom training, was to go out with me to my first 30 appointments and help me get started. In our first meeting, he told me about himself and how he had made the switch to this line of work as a second career after his previous employer laid him off. I told him about myself, my reasons for getting into the investment business, about my eyesight and how it made me want to find a new path. When he heard about my sight loss, he naturally had questions, one of which was, "Can you drive?" I said no.

"I think you're going to have a hard time succeeding in this business if you can't drive."

Ouch.

Working for that company meant being out of the office a lot trying to find clients and carrying a laptop everywhere I went. According to their IT people, their system would work with Zoom Text software. In this job, I was essentially an agent, meaning I made a commission on any clients I brought in who invested with the company and, as my book of business grew, I would get a small residual bonus each month. Being an agent also meant I had to buy my own computer, cover my own marketing costs and in my case, it meant I had to buy the Zoom Text software myself. Their tech support was not very helpful when it came to matters related to making the software work with their system, but after a few calls I was able to get their software and mine all up and running.

In late 2008, a friend of mine forwarded an email to me that he had received about a new government program called the Registered Disability Savings Plan (RDSP). His question was, "Is it legitimate?" Up to that point I had never heard of the RDSP, but I read the email and became both curious and excited at the same time.

On one hand, I was interested in opening my own RDSP and on the other hand, I thought if I could learn as much as possible about the program, it might be a great way to build my business, allowing me to help people with disabilities save for the future and be able to talk to them from the common ground of being someone with challenges myself.

The RDSP is a program meant to provide people with disabilities a source of income in their later years so they can be less reliant on other government social programs that, in some cases, come to an end once a person reaches retirement age. Without the RDSP, some people with disabilities end up losing their provincial disability support benefits, only to end up on CPP disability or welfare.

As I learned more about the RDSP, I went to the branch manager at my workplace and asked if the company was going to be offering the program to clients. He'd never heard of it and was leaving the branch; but the incoming manager asked for an analysis of why the company should offer such a program. I also created a spreadsheet showing the income potential of the program, including the very generous bonds and grants the government offered. With this information, both managers made inquiries for me with the head office. After a few weeks the answer came back, no. The head office of the company felt the target market for the RDSP was too small and the cost to roll out the program was too high. I was disappointed and thought it was very short sighted of the company to only look at the numbers and not realize the potential goodwill that could be gained. Plus, since it was about the numbers, I pointed out the lost potential business from the family members of the RDSP beneficiaries. He said he sympathised, but couldn't change the decision.

Life's Not Over, It Just Looks Different

The company's decision not to offer the RDSP was the last straw for me. I wasn't doing well at generating business; other things weren't happening the way I'd been told they would, and I found myself dreading the weekly rookie meetings. Finally, one day after having been on the job for only seven months, I decided I'd had enough. I told Cindy I was thinking of quitting and to my surprise she supported the idea.

"If I quit, there won't be any money coming in until I can find another job," I told her.

"There isn't any money coming in now," she replied. "If you quit, at least you won't be paying any money out." She was right. Since I was considered an agent with the company, I had a number of monthly expenses to cover and most months I had been with the firm I had paid them more than they'd paid me.

That night Cindy and I had plans to go out for dinner with some people we knew. As we walked from the car to the restaurant, I was dancing and feeling great. I felt like a huge weight had been lifted off my shoulders by quitting that job.

"You are the happiest person out of a job I have ever seen," Cindy said.

"I'm thrilled," I told her.

The first two months after leaving the consultant job were pretty quiet. I searched online, put in applications and tried connecting with people I knew in the financial services business to let them know I was looking again. Eventually, I started getting calls back and had a few phone interviews, but no offers. Tapping into as many available resources as I could, I also contacted an employment agency that specializes in helping people with disabilities find jobs. I had a chat with one of their placement staff and told him what I was looking for. My timing was good, because a week after meeting with him they happened to have a presentation going on where representatives from one of the big banks would be coming in to talk about opportunities at the bank and how to apply.

A few days later, I got a call from a recruiter who worked for a discount brokerage connected to the same bank whose website I had been on the previous week. She told me she had seen my résumé and asked if I was still looking for a new position. Wow, I thought, that was a quick response to the résumé I posted online. I told her I was, so we proceeded to have a brief phone interview. Her questions told me she had an older copy of my résumé, not the revised version I had posted online a few days earlier. That told me she had been given my name by one of the staff I knew at that bank. The old saying is true: it's about who you know. I went in for an interview a few days later.

At that interview, I met with the assistant branch manager and one of the team managers. With most job interviews, I normally wait for the ideal opportunity to talk about my eyesight, or wait for it to come up very naturally rather than just blurting it out. On that day however, I guess I was in a bit more of a "blurting" mood. I told the two interviewers early on that I was vision impaired and put my hand-held magnifier on the table in front of me. Once it was out in the open though, the conversation moved on and although I left the magnifier on the table the whole time, the subject of my sight never came up again.

About a week later, I received a call from another recruiter saying they were very interested in having me join them in the next training class.

A week before the class was to start, the brokerage called to set up a meeting to talk about the equipment I would need to do the job. We discussed various accommodations I'd need to do the job and some of the equipment, including the cost, like magnifying software, a CCTV and other devices I used at home. Anticipating some resistance to the cost of the equipment, I gave him some alternative ideas for devices like smaller portable CCTV units or perhaps printing materials off for me in large print so no device other than my hand-held magnifier would be needed.

"Tell me what you need and we'll make it happen," he said. I was floored!

I walked out of that meeting bursting with joy and wanting to tell somebody — anybody — how well they were treating me. On the way home, I passed by the offices of VoicePrint, so I stopped in to tell my friends there what a great meeting I'd just had and how receptive the bank was being to meeting my needs to do the job well. They were thrilled for me.

As planned, training for my new role as an investment representative at the discount brokerage began in June 2009. When I got to the class, I found a computer in the room loaded with the software and a large print keyboard at the ready. The role of investment representative was an in-bound call centre position. Once trained, I would be on the phone taking orders for a variety of investment products including stocks, mutual funds and options. It was also a customer service role, helping out with clients' questions or concerns related to their accounts.

Training didn't go quite as smoothly as I would've liked. Unfortunately, there was some issue between the magnifying software and the main software I needed to use for the job. The IT staff did their best, but couldn't make the two applications work together. Not wanting to appear high maintenance or pushy while I waited for the computer to be fixed, I did my best to persevere and used my hand-held magnifier to read the computer screen as best I could. It was challenging and tiring. At times, I found myself getting frustrated, because I felt like I was falling behind the class in learning some of the key job functions. To compensate, I went in early a few days and on the weekend to spend time with the computer and figure things out for myself. I was being treated well at the discount brokerage, aside from the computer problems, so I felt a little extra effort on my part would be worth it.

Life's Not Over, It Just Looks Different

In one of those odd computer quirks that sometimes make you wonder, "What on Earth is wrong?" the computer that had been set up for me on the trading floor worked just fine. There was no evidence of the issue that I faced in the training room. By all indications, it was exactly the same set up as the one in the training room, but somehow the one on the floor cooperated with the magnifying software, so I was able to function with no problems at what would become my desk once training was done. Although I was puzzled by what might be the difference between the two computers, the one I needed for the job worked, so I didn't argue with it.

I joined a team of ten people, in cubicles arranged in pairs of two, six rows deep. This allowed a newbie like me to have one person in front of me, one beside and another behind me who I could ask for assistance when I needed it. The best part for me was that my desk was next to two people I already knew in the office. That made settling in with my new team an easier task.

A DARK DAY

Working as an investment representative was a steep learning curve. Even with the four weeks of training, there was a lot to learn in a hurry, and I found out very quickly that the biggest unknown in the job was what the next client would ask me as I took each phone call. As I got more comfortable with the job, I began to embrace the uncertainty of each call, but in the early days, it was nerve wracking. I've come to realize that part of that was pressure I put on myself. I'm most comfortable in any role when I can recall things off the top of my head. Having to ask someone or needing to look up information makes any task more time consuming. Even as I began to see better to get around, processing information on paper or screens was still a slow process. I found it easier to memorize. And while I'm not afraid to ask questions, I prefer to be as self-reliant as possible — something I had to re-learn as I adjusted to working with the level of sight I had.

A month after training was complete and I was doing the job, I took a call one Wednesday afternoon and found myself in a situation that I really didn't understand and, as it turned out, never should have been involved with in the first place. I did ask questions, trying to find out how to handle the client's request, but apparently I wasn't asking the right people or the correct questions, because I wasn't getting a resolution. By Friday afternoon, it had turned into a bigger mess and one of the resource team members had to step in to resolve the situation. Resource was a team of people who helped mitigate issues and investigate problems with trades. Once the resource officer cleared up the issue for the client, he told me it was all worked out but that I shouldn't have been involved in the situation and, in what I felt was an ominous tone, he said, "Your manager will speak to you about it on Monday." I walked out of the office feeling doomed. The last words he said to me kept rolling around in my head and I was very worried. I thought for sure I would be fired on Monday.

That evening, I told Cindy what had happened and what the resource officer said. She tried to reassure me it was nothing to worry about and suggested we go to a movie. I agreed and we went to a nearby theatre. As I sat watching the movie, my head was still going over the events at work and my anxiety grew.

The next day I woke up still not feeling very good about the events of the previous few days. I couldn't shake the sense of impending doom I felt I was going to face on Monday. Cindy had gone to work that day, so she wasn't home to distract me from my thoughts. She called about noon to see how I was doing. I told her I still felt bad about work. The night before, we had talked about my need for some new dress shoes and she suggested we go to the mall when she was done her shift.

About two hours later, still moping and dreading the start of the coming week, I decided I just didn't want to be there anymore.

I packed a duffle bag with a few clothes and some writing pads, my iPod and my passport and headed out the door. I walked down the street, hopped on the bus, down to the subway station and rode the

169

trains to the last stop on the Yonge subway line; the farthest point Toronto's subway went north. From there I started walking north on Yonge Street.

But where was I going?

I had a vague idea about going home, to northwest Ontario, back to my hometown of Atikokan. By car, it was about a nineteen-hour drive from Toronto. I had no idea how long it would be on foot. Was I really going to walk that far? Probably not, but at that point, my main thought was just to get away.

As I walked up Yonge, it began to rain and, although I had packed a change of clothes in my duffle bag, one thing I hadn't brought with me was a jacket or raincoat. The farther I walked, the harder the rain came down. At times, the gusts of wind made the rain even more intense, but I wasn't going to be stopped by the downpour. After one rather strong gust, I looked up into the sky and said, somewhat audibly, "No matter how hard it rains, I'm not going to stop," and continued to walk, even more determined than before.

Somewhere north of Newmarket, the town immediately north of Toronto, the sidewalks ended and now I was walking on the shoulder of the highway approaching Bradford. I crossed the street to the left, then back to the right, then back to the left side, ultimately deciding it was better to face oncoming traffic, even if it meant I couldn't see all the road signs.

Life's Not Over, It Just Looks Different

Darkness fell about 8 p.m. Walking on the shoulder of the road was challenging, because the gravel was rough and it was tough to see where I was stepping. I was doing my best not to step in any potholes or other ruts along the side of the road, but at the same time I didn't want to walk too close to the side of the road and risk being hit by an oncoming vehicle. A few times I guess I got a little too close to the road for the drivers' liking and was honked at.

Out there alone with no one to talk to and the battery in my iPod having been exhausted, I went over the mistake I had made on the job and how nervous I was at the thought of being fired. At the time, all I could think was, what would I do if I lost that job? What else could I do? What other business could I work in with my bad eyesight?

No answers came, and I just kept putting one foot in front of the other.

With a pang of regret, I thought about Cindy. I knew it was selfish to run away. On the other hand, I told myself, "She'll make it without me." At times I wanted to call her, but I knew we would both just break down in tears. Besides, if I phoned her, I'd eventually have to hang up in order to keep going. I couldn't decide which was harder; resisting the temptation to call Cindy or the scenario playing out in my head where I would call her and we'd both be in tears as I hung up the phone to keep walking.

I was determined not to go home. I really wanted to get lost. I decided I would write Cindy a note to let her know how I felt and what had made me walk away. I wasn't sure when I was going to send it, or where I would send the letter from.

For now, I just wanted to keep walking.

Somewhere near Bradford, I started looking for a place to sit down and write the note. It was close to 9 p.m., and I needed a place with enough light to see the paper. I have trouble reading my own handwriting at the best of times and writing in the dark was even harder. I eventually came across a business with a lighted portable sign in front that I thought would provide enough light. I sat on a large stone in front of the sign and started to write. It was the first time I had sat down since beginning my walk. The rain had stopped, too, so at least I had a dry place to sit.

"Dear Cindy," I began. "First things first, I am really sorry…"

I poured out my fears to her — losing my job because of the incident at work and having to find some other way to earn money. At one point, I told her she'd be better off without me dragging her down. Although most days I truly believed I was going to overcome any challenge the vision impairment presented, in the past 36 hours, my normal "fight" response had been replaced with a "flight" response: I was literally trying to get as far away as I could from the fear of total failure.

I wrote until there was nothing more to write, and started off again down Highway 11, which picked up where Yonge Street left off and would lead me to my hometown — eventually.

Life's Not Over, It Just Looks Different

Ahead of me lay northwest Ontario; a place of natural beauty, with lakes, forests and rocky surfaces; it had been a great place to grow up. Images of climbing the rocks with friends, catching frogs in the pond near our house and exploring the trails in the wooded areas took me back to a simpler time and a place of unspoiled beauty. The memories soothed the turmoil I was feeling inside, and helped me to keep going.

Walking through Bradford, I was relieved to have sidewalks to walk on instead of the uneven surface of the gravel shoulder. Once I left, however, I had to resort to walking along the roadside. Leaving Bradford also meant I was once again in pitch darkness. My legs were cramping up, and I was soaked from head to toe from the earlier rain. My clothes were sticking to my body, and my feet began to hurt as I walked on the rocky surface of the highway shoulder.

By midnight, I was tired, sore and didn't want to navigate the gravel shoulder of the road in the dark any longer. I needed a place to bed down. I would wait for daylight when I could see the walking surface more clearly. About six kilometres north of Bradford I came upon a highway overpass, climbed over the guard rail and found a relatively flat spot on the dirt to lie down. I had been walking for almost eight hours and, other than being six kilometres north of Bradford, which I'd seen on a highway sign, I really had no idea how far I had walked.

I also hadn't eaten much since leaving home that afternoon and began to feel sick to my stomach. The feeling passed after a few dry heaves, but getting comfortable on the slope under the overpass was something else. No matter which way I tried to position my legs, they hurt — cramps from too much walking, and now spasms trying to rest on ground too cold to soothe the cramps. I contorted myself in a few different ways and managed to settle down using my duffle bag as a pillow, but I couldn't sleep.

With nothing to distract me now, I couldn't help but deal with what was going on in my head. I was sure Cindy would be worried and wondering where I was, and I felt guilty about running away. I was so lucky to have her in my life. She had stood by me through so much over the 12 years we'd been together, and now I'd disappeared without a word to her. But when I remembered why, the obsessive worrying about work took over, and I told myself I still couldn't go home. As soon as it was light out, I would continue on my way. Somewhere along the way, I would send Cindy the note.

Between the wet clothes, aching legs and the rumbling of large trucks on the other side of the guard rail, I only got about two hours of light rest. I never did fully relax.

All I managed to do was debate continuing, or going back. Neither was going to be easy. My stubbornness was still running strong, and I kept telling myself I had to keep going — until I would, once again, start thinking about Cindy and what this was doing to her. She loved me! Why was I hurting her like this? I broke down in tears, out of sight and still under the cover of darkness. About 3 a.m., I finally decided to start walking home. I climbed back over the guard rail and started back on the same path I'd taken to get to that spot. My legs were killing me; every step took a lot of effort and my feet ached so much, it felt like there was almost nothing between them and the gravel shoulder. With each step, I wondered if I was even going to make it home. Although I had finally realized that running away was not an option, I now realized that getting home might also be an impossible task. To top it off, I was thirsty. I hoped to find a stream somewhere along the way, but all there was, was a ditch filled with yesterday's rain water.

I walked off the shoulder toward the ditch and pulled a travel mug from my bag to scoop up some water. The ditch was muddy and my footing was not very secure, so I moved slowly, trying not to fall in. I was pretty sure I wouldn't have the strength to pull myself out.

As careful as I was not to scoop up any mud, the water tasted terrible. It kept me going, though, until I found a gas station where I bought a chocolate bar and bottle of juice.

As I trudged along, I felt so weak, it seemed I might collapse at any moment. I told myself there was no way I was going to be able to walk as far as I had the day before, so I began looking for a transit stop that might get me home. But would the buses even be running this early on a Sunday? I decided to find a transit stop first and then worry about that later. If nothing else, I'd have a place to sit and rest my tired legs and feet.

It took about three hours' walking, but I reached a transit stop. The next bus was in 20 minutes, and I didn't know where it was going, but I decided to wait anyway, because even if that bus couldn't take me closer to home, at least I'd be able to ask where to get a bus that would.

The bus was right on time and it was going to Finch station in Toronto — perfect!

I sat down on a seat near the front. I was so relieved that I could stop walking, I no longer cared about the problem that had made me run away in the first place. I came to the conclusion that if I got fired the next day, so be it. I'd find something else. I had allowed my self-confidence to be shaken by the events at work.

The bus pulled into the subway station about 7 a.m. Now, just two trains and another bus to get home. Once on the bus, I fought to stay awake. I was so tired; it would've been easy to fall asleep right there.

I got off at my stop, crossed the road and started walking down our street toward the condo. I wondered what would greet me. Was Cindy upset, mad, just glad to have me home safe and sound — or would I be in serious trouble?

I limped down our street, my feet still aching from the walk and my legs still very stiff with each step. About a block from home, a police car going the opposite direction stopped and backed up. One of the officers waved me over to the car.

Life's Not Over, It Just Looks Different

"Are you Christopher Warner?" he asked. I nodded. "Did you know you've been reported missing?" I dropped my head into my chest and started to cry.

The officers put me in the back of the car to take me home and radioed dispatch to say they'd found their missing person. The other officer asked me where I had gone. I told him, Bradford.

"Bradford? How did you get there?"

"I took transit part of the way and walked the rest."

"You walked all the way to Bradford?" the officer asked, wide-eyed. I nodded. Bradford was nearly 50 kilometres north of Toronto's last subway stop.

One of the officers called Cindy to tell her they found me, and the three of us went to the condo to wait for her.

Inside the condo, the officers asked me why I had disappeared. I told them about the situation at work, what the resource officer said and how I was scared about the outcome. They both tried to reassure me that they didn't think it would be as bad as I feared.

As we talked, the other officer asked if he could search my duffle bag. He pulled out one of my note pads to look through it and said to the other officer, "I see the words suicide and life insurance policy written here."

"Those are my notes from my life insurance training. I'm licensed to sell life insurance," I replied, before they could go any further. He continued to look through my note pads and found the note to Cindy.

Cindy arrived at the condo a few minutes later with two of our friends coming in behind her. She looked across the room at me sitting on the couch and said "Hi" in a gentle tone. I got up from the couch and walked over to give her a hug. I told her I was sorry and broke into tears again. She told me she was just glad I was okay. The officers showed Cindy the note I had written for her and said they wanted to take me to the hospital to have me checked out.

At the hospital, the officers told the nurse what happened and that I should probably be seen by the trauma team. The trauma team checked me out and then referred me to the psychiatrist on call.

Sitting in the examining room we talked about what had happened since Friday. The doctor held up the note I'd written on my way and said that if he was to read between the lines it sounded like a suicide note. I told him I'd written it when I was convinced I wasn't coming back.

"Where were you going?" he asked. I told him I was heading back to my hometown near Thunder Bay. He stopped to process that for a moment, and then he asked, "Did you really think you were going to make it?"

Life's Not Over, It Just Looks Different

"That was the goal," I told him, but then added that with the pain my legs and feet were feeling it became clear it was going to be tough.

He asked if I had ever seen a psychiatrist and I told him I saw one regularly. He said he wouldn't keep me in the hospital but strongly recommended I call my own doctor ASAP. Then he sent me home with some pills to help me relax.

Back at home, I took off my shoes for the first time in about 24 hours. My feet started to swell almost immediately and the blisters on the bottom were massive. Cindy and I decided the best thing was to pop the blisters and let the skin start healing. She gently pricked each blister with a pin and then put a towel under my feet to soak up the draining fluid.

As the blisters on my feet slowly drained, Cindy and I talked. I was relieved to be home, but wracked with guilt over my actions. I think I apologized to her more than a dozen times for what I had put her through by running away. She stayed very calm; she was just glad to have me home. I apologized again, to which Cindy responded, "You went crazy for a while and now you're back."

I woke up the next morning and went to work as normal, not telling anyone in the office about how I'd spent my weekend. I was still limping from the blisters on my feet, but it must not have been too obvious because no one asked about it.

Later that day I had a chat with my manager about the events from the previous week. He'd heard about it, but only commented that no real harm had been done, but that until I was fully licensed, I should pass things like that on to a manager. With that, the issue was closed.

I had really overreacted and caused a lot of pain and suffering for myself and those around me for nothing. I suddenly realized that although I thought I had adjusted well to my new level of sight, and it might have appeared so to others, there was obviously part of me that was insecure and not at ease with this lifestyle change yet.

Life's Not Over, It Just Looks Different

CREATING A NICHE

In November 2009, the discount brokerage began offering RDSP accounts to its clients. Having spent a lot of time studying the RDSP before I joined the company, I was excited about having the opportunity to share information about the program with clients.

I let my managers know how happy I was that the company was getting on board with the program and how much I wanted to help promote it. Initially, only the members of my team were coming to me with questions about the RDSP and, as the months progressed, a few more team managers in the office began directing their team members to me when RDSP questions came up. It wasn't that the program was overly complicated or that there wasn't enough information available through the internal resources. In fact, the opposite was true. There was so much information available to the investment representatives, it was overwhelming at first.

By March 2010, word had spread about my interest in the RDSP. I did an interview at VoicePrint for their weekly interview show. And soon after, another division of the bank asked me to do a presentation on the RDSP and TFSA to a group at the CNIB. I worked with two members of the product development department, so they could be confident in what I was going to say and that I would cover any points they wanted to focus on. I also saw this as an opportunity to make sure others in the organization knew about my passion for the program and that I was eager to speak to any groups who asked about it.

After the interview and the presentation, opportunities to speak about the RDSP didn't come around again until about a year later, when I was able to talk about RDSPs with groups of new investment reps who were joining the discount brokerage. A few months earlier, I had asked the training facilitator in our office if he had incorporated the RDSP into his training of the new reps. He hadn't, and so I told him I was more than happy to speak about it.

Being known as a subject matter expert on the RDSP program for most of the three years I was with the discount brokerage was a fun experience. The RDSP was a small niche I was able to carve out for myself but, unlike other roles in the company where there might be competition from other staff, the RDSP was a niche that nobody else seemed to want to get in on, which left it to me and I was fine with that.

A hidden disability

I don't like to think of myself as disabled, and I really dislike the word handicapped. I prefer to think of myself as having challenges. That's part of the reason I stopped using a white cane about two years after it had been given to me.

It's a decision that has produced some interesting responses — even in my own family.

Life's Not Over, It Just Looks Different

In Toronto's underground path system, a network of underground walkways that allows a person to cover a lot of downtown Toronto without going outside, I was trying to follow the signs to one of the subway stations one day. I couldn't find it on my own and decided to ask the clerk at a small newsstand if he could point me to the subway. Although I don't see faces very well, I often pick up on people's facial expressions. As the clerk pointed to the subway sign, which, as it turned out was right behind me, he looked incredulous and a bit skeptical. Once I explained that I was vision impaired, his tone completely changes. "Oh, sorry," he said. "I didn't know. It's right over there."

A few days before Christmas, December 2007, Cindy and I were flying to Winnipeg for the holidays. In the airport before boarding the plane, Cindy and I were in the bookstore because she wanted to pick up a magazine for the flight. While I waited for her, I was picking up different books and reading the back covers with my magnifier. I read the description of one that sounded interesting and was just putting it down when Cindy came over to me.

"That sounds like an interesting book," I said to her.

"So get it."

I thought, sure why not and went to pay for it, thinking to myself I wasn't sure I wanted to read the book with a hand-held magnifying glass, so it might have to wait until we returned home.

On the plane a short time later, I decided I did want to read the book after all, so I took it out of our carry-on bag and began reading it with my magnifying glass. Cindy looked at me and said "Oh right, I forgot you had to read it with your magnifier."

"How did you think I was going to read it?"

"Like normal people," she replied.

Her comment surprised me and at the same time made me feel good, because it meant that she didn't see me as disabled. I had wondered about that from time to time, and it was nice to know she sometimes forgets about my condition and sees me as "normal."

Two weeks before Cindy's revelation during our trip, about fourteen months after the surgery, I went to see the ophthalmologist for an annual assessment. My visual field test was a wash, as it had been the time before, but I went through the motions with the lab assistant because the only doctor's note I had said my progress would be assessed in one year. In the lab outside the doctor's office, the technician set up the test for my right eye and we started the procedure. A few seconds passed and she noticed I wasn't clicking on the mouse to signify I was seeing the sparks on the test. She asked if I was okay and I told her I was fine; I was just waiting to see the sparks.

With the test of the right eye complete, she set me up to start testing the left eye and asked if I was ready to begin. I told her I was and she started the test. After about 30 seconds, again she told me to start. And

Life's Not Over, It Just Looks Different

again I told her I was waiting for the sparks to begin where I could see them. She was a bit surprised and let out a little giggle.

I discovered two things about how my sight was affected by the drops in my eyes that day. First, the world was much brighter for me than normal but not to the point where I needed to shield my eyes or squint like I used to when my pupils were dilated. And second, in the past the drops made my sight fuzzy for a while, but apparently my sight is so bad, I could barely notice the increased blurriness from the drops!

In addition to a small comedy of lowered expectations with the lab tech, who didn't seem to understand that being vision impaired meant I couldn't see the little sparks of light (I am missing entire sections of the visual field), the ophthalmologist told me my left eye had shifted slightly off centre, a common side effect of pressure from hydrocephalus. There was a very routine procedure he could do and it would be covered by my government health plan. Well, we all know what happened with the last "routine procedure," too — my shunt revision. When I reminded him of that fact, he wisely admitted I might be a little uneasy about going for any surgical procedures after what had taken place in 2005, and left it up to me.

He quickly changed the topic to work, specifically asking if I was back at work yet, so I told him what had happened with the TV station and about my job as a studio producer with VoicePrint.

"Well," he said, "I'm pleased to see you adjusting to your new level of sight."

"Well, doctor, I'd still rather have my full sight back, but if that's not possible, I'm going to do what I can to carry on."

"Are you still using the white cane to get around?" he asked, valiantly trying to get the conversation back on an even keel.

"No, I don't need it."

"Maybe you should, though, especially when crossing the street. Drivers won't be aware you have a problem navigating the crosswalk if they don't see that cane."

I just grinned and said, "The way people drive these days, carrying the white cane won't stop them from hitting me. It'll just let them know they hit a blind guy!"

Like the ophthalmologist, other doctors also told me I should use the white cane so people would know I may need assistance. I think about it differently. Not using the cane was my way of getting my independence back. I've been self-sufficient most of my life and I decided that I didn't want reduced eyesight to change that if I could help it.

One summer day in 2010, on the way to a Toronto area hospital I was familiar with for an appointment, I got turned around and couldn't find my way. I knew it was close, but I needed help, so I stopped a man walking toward me and asked him where the hospital was. He turned to face the same direction I was looking, pointed to a large building about a block away and said, "Big H," with a quizzical grin on his face. I pulled out my monocular and focused on the top of the building he pointed to and said, "Oh yeah, there it is!"

His mouth fell open, and I felt the need to explain.

"I'm vision impaired," I said, "and have trouble seeing that far."

More funny moments

Without the white cane, my lack of sight provides great material for Toastmaster speeches.

One of my favourites was "White Cane Chronicles" where I told stories of humorous experiences both with the cane and without. I opened the speech by taking out my white cane, taking off the strap and letting it unfold itself in front of the audience. It makes a noticeable clicking sound as the elastic in the cane causes the individual segments to unfold and snap into place. Anyone not paying attention at that moment "snaps to" in a hurry! I must be very convincing without the cane, because once the speech was over, a man in the audience whom I had met just a few weeks earlier and who apparently didn't know about my condition, came up to me and said when I first pulled out the white cane, he thought the speech was all an act!

In the summer of 2012, a bus shelter was being constructed at my normal bus stop near work. This meant that for a few days the temporary stop was a little further down the road while the concrete pad was poured and the shelter assembled. Not realizing the stop had been moved, I stood in the usual spot and waited for the bus. Another passenger, a lady, did the same thing. Even though we weren't standing at the temporary stop, the driver was kind enough to stop and pick us up. As the other passenger got on the bus ahead of me, the driver barked, "This is not the stop. Didn't you see the sign? The stop is over there," and she pointed out the front window of the bus. Then, I climbed on and showed my CNIB card and transit pass.

"Oh," said the driver, touching my elbow, "but you're forgiven."

And then there was the time in 2010 when I had to renew my driver's licence. No, that's not a misprint. I renewed my driver's licence.

I had previously renewed it in early October 2005, just a few weeks before I'd gone in for surgery. During the follow up visits with the various doctors, the subject of my driver's licence just never came up. In Ontario, licences are renewed every five years, so I wasn't going to have to worry about it until October 2010.

I was glad the doctors didn't pull my licence, because it's still a very useful piece of photo ID.

Occasionally, I use my CNIB card, but a driver's licence is the one piece of ID, other than a passport, that nobody quarrels with.

As October 2010 rolled around, I anticipated the arrival of the renewal form. When it showed up in our mailbox, I filled it out anyway, even though I was sure I would be denied. On the form, there was a question that asked, "Is there anything that might inhibit your ability to drive?" In total honesty, in large block letters, I printed LEGALLY BLIND. I went to the renewal office in downtown Toronto and waited in line. When it was my turn at the counter, I handed the customer service agent my renewal form and my credit card. He took the form, processed my payment and said nothing about what I had written on it. Two weeks later, my new driver's licence arrived in the mail.

Since I was no longer using the white cane, no one questioned it when I showed my licence as a piece of identification. Until one day at the bank, when I wanted to make a change to one of my accounts. The representative helping me out knew who I was and also knew about my sight. When she asked for two pieces of ID to add to the account application, I handed her my licence and birth certificate. She took them both and walked toward the photocopier, when she suddenly stopped, turned back to me and asked, "How does a vision impaired guy have a driver's licence?" When I told her how, she laughed right out loud.

NEW HOME, NEW TURF AND NEW ADVENTURES

By the spring of 2012, Cindy and I had been living in Toronto for a little over 12 years. Living in Canada's biggest city all those years gave us the opportunity to do some cool things, try a wide variety of foods, thanks to the city's cultural diversity and most importantly, meet many great people. For me, though, the city itself never really felt like home. We lived in a great neighbourhood with a lot of things close by, but if we had to venture downtown or to other parts of the city, its size and the extra travel time were issues that bothered me. I often describe Toronto as "too big, too busy, too crowded and too smoggy." Over the years I'd suggested to Cindy that we look for jobs somewhere else, like Winnipeg or Calgary. Each time she said no — she liked our condo, and Toronto winters were much milder than in places like Winnipeg or Regina when we lived there. Eventually though, it was the smog that drove us out when Cindy developed breathing problems.

One day in March 2012, Cindy came home and told me she was applying for a posting in Calgary through the company she worked for.

"Cool," I said. "When are we leaving?"

I had fallen in love with the city of Calgary the first time I visited it in 1993. I liked the energy of the city, its proximity to the mountains and the many green spaces. Most of all, I was a big fan of the city's pro football team, the Calgary Stampeders. Right from that first visit, I knew I wanted to live there someday, so Cindy's announcement that she was interested in applying for a job in my favourite city was music to my ears! She got the job, agreeing to start in early April.

I had been working for the discount brokerage for almost three years, but I knew that moving to Calgary would mean finding a new position because the same job didn't exist with the bank for me to do a direct transfer. With the number of financial courses I had taken by that time and the experience gained, I hoped it wouldn't be too hard to find a job in Calgary. Surely somebody in Calgary needs help with their finances, I thought.

Cindy and I went to Calgary the weekend before she started her new job, so I could help her get settled in. We spent the weekend visiting her cousins and, first thing Monday morning, Cindy began training for her new job. It just so happened that the downtown Calgary location of the company I worked for had an opening posted just before I went out, so I was able to arrange an in-person interview while I was there on the Monday afternoon, before I had to fly back to Toronto. I wasn't offered the job, but it was worth a shot.

Truthfully, not getting a job in Calgary right away myself was a good thing. It meant we were less rushed to get our condo sold and all of our stuff packed. I also had surgery booked on my ankle for late April, which was going to have me on crutches for about six weeks, so it was better I stayed in Toronto for a while.

One thing I quickly learned about being on crutches was how tiring it was. Being unable to drive, I walked a lot anyway and adding crutches, or as I called them "the twins," just added a new element of challenge to my walks to work, the mall and the grocery store. During those six weeks of walking with the twins I was glad I didn't need to use a white cane, because I didn't have a hand available to hold it.

We decided I would join Cindy in Calgary at the beginning of July. Everything worked pretty much as planned. The condo sold in June, and the movers came about a week before I was scheduled to leave Toronto. For that last week, the cat and I "roughed it" with just a few essentials until it was time to catch our flight.

Being the football fan I am, I timed my arrival in Calgary on Canada Day, so that I had enough time to drop off my stuff at our new apartment and head to the Stampeders' season-opening football game later that day.

My first two months in Calgary were about getting the lay of the land. I had to figure out my neighbourhood and change the address on all my identification. I also needed to change my CNIB card and was hoping to get some assistance from the staff about getting around Calgary. I was having no luck finding a job, either through the bank I worked for or online. Tapping into any resource I could think of, I also spoke to the CNIB about some job search help. Although the staff I met with were very nice and easy to talk to, I learned that they were facing budget cutbacks and were losing their own jobs very soon. I felt bad asking them to help me find a job when the two of them were losing theirs.

Having moved to Calgary in the summer, I had great weather most days to get out and walk around to explore my new surroundings. One helpful thing about Calgary is that the area we first lived in and the downtown area both had mostly numbered streets. The city is also divided into quadrants, so that made it a little easier to find my way around. Plus, I figured out that the odd numbered addresses were on the south side of the east-west routes and the west side of the north-south roads, which made it a little easier to get around.

Even with that information in my back pocket, so to speak, I still found ways to get lost from time to time. I hadn't figured out the transit system right away and didn't get to know the bus or LRT routes in the first few weeks, preferring to travel mostly on foot. It was time consuming to travel that way when I could have caught a bus or train, but figuring things out on foot had its advantages. Walking everywhere for the first couple of months allowed me to get up close to buildings or signage I wanted to check out and, because I wasn't passing by things quickly on a transit bus or train, I had more time to really absorb my environment.

A few times in the first month I did get lost, which sometimes caused moments of self doubt and anxiety. One particular day, I posted my frustration on Facebook, sharing the self doubt I was feeling about adjusting to a new city with my friends and family. The comments that came back were words of encouragement and messages to boost my confidence, which really helped. Words weren't going to keep me from getting lost, but their thoughts and messages helped to shift my thinking back to a more positive frame of mind about my ability to overcome the challenges of learning our new city.

Between my smart phone, which had a good map, and Calgary Transit, I got much more comfortable in the first two months. The trains had stop announcements to let me know where I was, and bus drivers could usually be persuaded to call out my stop.

Finding my way around the city that first summer dovetailed with my job search. If a posting looked interesting, the first thing I did was check on a map to see how easily I could get there. If it didn't look like an easy commute, or if it looked like it would take too much time to commute one way, I didn't bother applying.

In the first two months not much happened for me. Nothing had come out of a meeting I had with the HR department at the bank I'd worked for in Toronto, and I didn't put any pressure on the two people I had met at the CNIB, because they had their own job searches to worry about. While I was looking, I also decided to look into taking some courses or volunteering, and found both. One of the local universities had a program to become an adult educator. I liked training and coaching people in my previous jobs, so that seemed like a good thing to study further.

Life's Not Over, It Just Looks Different

I had been volunteering as part of a debt counselling clinic with a local non-profit in Toronto, and when it became clear I was moving to Calgary, my contact there gave me the name of an organization in Calgary that she said had similar programs and suggested I call them. I followed up on it when I got to Calgary and was told that they didn't need any volunteers for their financial literacy programs, but they asked if I would be interested in volunteering as an English language tutor. That sounded interesting, so I signed up.

It never fails that once one thing is in place, other things start popping up, forcing us to make choices. I continued to look for employment while starting a couple of volunteer jobs and in early September, as I started my third month in Calgary, calls for job interviews started to come in.

The first interview was with a bank. Not the same one I worked with in Toronto, but another of Canada's big six banks. The interview went well. I told the two managers in the meeting about my vision impairment and the devices I would need to perform the job. I was told that would be no problem; the bank was capable of accommodating my needs, and the hiring manager concluded the interview saying he'd call me later in the week to let me know their decision.

Later that same week, I got an interview with a non-profit agency for a position as a credit counsellor. I told the hiring manager about my vision impairment. She stopped, looked at me, looked at her computer screen and then back at me. The job involved a lot of work using a computer, but I told her about the devices available to help me do that, and she offered to speak with the company president to see if they could accommodate my needs, should I be hired.

I left that interview with mixed emotions. I really liked the hiring manager and felt she'd be good to work with. I also really wanted to take on the role of credit counsellor, because I had enjoyed doing it on a volunteer basis in Toronto — getting paid for it would be even better.

My only reluctance about the job came up during the discussion about my sight and the devices to help me do the job. Although I really liked the idea of being a credit counsellor, I felt that by taking the job, I would not only have to learn the role but would also have the added responsibility of fighting for the cause of the vision impaired in the workplace.

During the discussion, we also talked about the cost of the devices. To smooth the way on this point, I negotiated a deal where they would cover the cost of the software and half of the CCTV, which I purchased myself. If I successfully completed one year of employment, they would reimburse me for the other half of the CCTV.

A few days later, after some calls back and forth with both the non-profit organization and the hiring manager at the bank, who had also called to offer me a job, I decided to take the credit counselling role with the non-profit.

Life's Not Over, It Just Looks Different

THE FOURTEENTH SURGERY

When I was a kid, shunt revisions were done almost annually as I grew, until 1980 when the doctor put in extra catheter for me to "grow into." As an adult, shunt surgeries have been unexpected events. The neurosurgeon who performed the 2001 and 2005 surgeries had said he did not want to do the operation unnecessarily, because there was too great a risk of complications or infection. In light of what happened in 2005, he was right.

The neurosurgeon's opinion was shared by his successor at Sunnybrook in Toronto. I first met the new surgeon in 2010. I had fainted at work and, in an effort to rule out every possible problem, our family doctor referred me to him for a check on the shunt. It had been nearly five years since the surgery, so a check up was probably a good idea.

I had a CT scan of my head before my first meeting with the surgeon. Later in his office, as he looked at the results of the scan on his computer, he pointed to a large dark area on my brain scan and said, "Looking at this area here, I'd swear you were blind."

He obviously hadn't read any notes on my history at that hospital.

"It's funny you say that." I said. "I am legally blind. What you see on that scan happened during my last shunt revision."

I filled him in on the story of the last surgery; he agreed with the previous neurosurgeon and said he, too, didn't want to do unnecessary surgery for exactly the same reasons.

He did tell me, however, that if I ever felt any pain in my head that felt like more than a normal headache, I was to go straight to emergency. He said it was obvious I was very dependent on the shunt and shouldn't play around with it. Even if it turned out to be nothing, it was better to be safe than sorry.

Two years later, Cindy and I moved to Calgary, so that was the only time I saw that doctor in Toronto.

Being in a new city meant finding new doctors and other services, hopefully as close to home as possible. It took a few months for Cindy and I to get established with a new family doctor and in one of my first meetings with her, I asked which hospital was the best place for me to go in case I needed help with my shunt. My experience with the hospitals in Toronto taught me this was a good question to ask so I could try to avoid going to a hospital that didn't deal with neurosurgical cases. She told me Foothills hospital in northwest Calgary was the place to be if anything went wrong with the shunt.

Fast forward to March, 2013. Cindy and I had been living in Calgary for nearly a year.

I was feeling fine and thought if my family doctor wanted some history on it besides what was in the records I had brought with me from

Toronto, she would ask. For the time being, I knew which hospital to go to if I had a problem, and that was good enough for me.

Now, a shunt failure is unpredictable and has different ways of making its presence known. When I woke up one Monday morning in March, I initially felt fine. I went to an appointment with the chiropractor that morning, which lasted about 15 minutes, and then walked the short distance to our apartment. Back at home though, I began feeling ill. About 10 a.m. I felt a bit of a headache. I decided it might be from lack of sleep, so I crawled back into bed and slept for about two hours.

When I woke up the headache was still with me, so I took a pain pill. Long after it should've kicked in, I still didn't feel right. Cindy sent a text and asked how I was doing. I said I had a headache. She asked if it was one of "those" headaches. I sent back a text saying I wasn't sure, but would keep her posted. Two more hours passed and I began to notice I was feeling a little extra sensitive to light in the room. Cindy called me for an update. I told her I still had the headache and now, light sensitivity. She said I didn't sound good, either. According to her, I was slow to respond to her questions and seemed to be struggling with my sentences. I told her I still wasn't sure what I was dealing with and I'd let her know if it got any worse. After she hung up, I called Alberta's telephone health line. Much like the service in Ontario, the telephone health line is staffed by nurses who can provide guidance over the phone based on symptoms reported by patients who call in.

"I have a VP shunt and I'm not sure if I am having a shunt failure, but I want to run my symptoms by you," I said to the nurse on the phone. She listened to my symptoms and asked a few routine questions to rule out other possible conditions.

"Based on the criteria you've given me, you're coming up on my screen as urgent," she said. "That means you should get to the hospital within four hours."

"Okay," I said.

"That doesn't mean wait four hours before going to hospital. You should go there now in case it's a lengthy wait in emergency."

"My wife will be home in about two hours," I said. "I'll have her take me."

"I wouldn't wait that long, if you can avoid it," she said.

I called Cindy to tell her what the nurse said. She arranged to get off work early and came home, a short drive from her workplace.

The EMS team arrived a short time later. Cindy told them about my shunt and said we were told by our family doctor that if I had a shunt problem I should go to Foothills hospital. But that wasn't how it worked in Alberta. The policy was to go to the hospital with the shortest wait time to have the patient seen as quickly as possible.

Life's Not Over, It Just Looks Different

At the hospital, it didn't take long to realize the staff there wasn't very familiar with VP shunts. It took a few hours to get a CT scan and, after reviewing it, the emergency room doctor said she didn't see anything wrong on the scan, or in my eyes. It sounded like she was going to send me home. Instead, they made a call to Foothills and arrangements were made to transfer me there.

Seven hours after arriving at the first hospital, I was finally transported to the hospital I had asked to go to in the first place. Luckily for me, because this was a direct transfer from another hospital, the neurosurgery department had someone waiting for me when I arrived. The surgical resident who saw me shortly after I arrived quickly confirmed my shunt was not functioning properly and that I would need surgery.

Once admitted to the NICU ward, the circus began in earnest. Because I was not acute, I would merely be "on call" for surgery, meaning I was not allowed to eat from midnight each night until a decision was made the next day about whether or not I was going in for surgery.

The following day, Tuesday, they brought me a lunch tray — no surgery today, so I was allowed to eat.

That afternoon, a neurosurgeon came by. He'd seen the scans of my brain from the night before and was trying to decide on the best course of action. The tests showed that the blockage appeared to be in the proximal catheter that went from the ventricles of the brain to the shunt reservoir. Given this, he felt there were three possible options.

Plan A was to replace the small portion of the catheter at the top of the shunt system. Plan B involved replacing the whole system from the ventricles of the brain all the way down to the bottom end in the pleural cavity near my right lung.

He stopped and asked, "Why was the shunt routed to that part of my body?" He said it was unusual to put it there when the normal location was to put it in the peritoneal cavity. In fact, he said he had only seen one or two other patients with the shunt draining near the lung, like mine. I gave him a short version of what took place to cause the previous surgeon to choose that location, and he replied that if he felt plan B was necessary (replace the whole system) he was inclined to put the shunt back in my lower right abdomen, where it had been for many years.

And then there was plan C, the one that would take the most work. Plan C would be to replace the entire shunt and catheter system, but route the entire thing down the left side of my body. He said he would know better once they opened me up and got a look at what was really going on with the shunt.

I started to thank him for stopping by, but as I did, I had to stop and catch my breath before I could get the words out. It was so refreshing

Life's Not Over, It Just Looks Different

to have a doctor provide such a complete explanation of what he saw and how he planned to deal with it.

Wednesday was another surgical let down, but at least there was lunch! About ten minutes later, the nurse came back and asked how much I had eaten.

"Not much," I said.

"The doctor says he has a spot for you at the end of the day, so you have to stop eating now, because we need eight hours of non-eating to take you in."

I looked at the food tray in front of me, looked back at the nurse and said, "Can I at least finish the can of Coke Cindy just brought me?"

"If you finish it quickly, I didn't see it," said the nurse.

False alarm. They brought me a dinner tray around five o'clock that afternoon. So much for Wednesday!

On Thursday, I found out around noon there would be no surgery that day either. I had now been in hospital almost four full days and started having doubts. Was I really sick enough? Was it a false alarm? I was certainly having headaches but hadn't been nauseated, which is usually another clear sign of a shunt problem, so I started to think maybe I should go home.

That night I had trouble sleeping and thought more and more about how long I had been waiting. If they told me I wasn't going in for surgery on Friday, I was going to check myself out of the hospital. When the nurse came by that morning, she asked how I was doing.

"I'm not having a good day. If they tell me I'm not going in for surgery today, they'd better bring me a therapist," I told her.

"Hopefully today will be your day," she said.

A resident came to see me about noon and brought bad news. I wasn't going in for surgery that day. I didn't protest, didn't lash out or even cry, despite being very frustrated at the news. Instead, I went for a walk.

As I walked down the hall past the nurses' station, one of the nurses greeted me. "Hi, Mr. Warner. You likely don't remember me, but I was your nurse earlier in the week. How are you doing?"

"I'm not having a good day. I was just told I'm not going in for surgery again today." And I kept walking toward the end of the hall.

At the end of the hall, I stopped at the double doors that would have been my exit from the ward and stared at them for a minute or two, then turned and started walking back the other way. As I passed by the nurses' station again, the same nurse called out, "Mr. Warner, you're going in for surgery today."

Life's Not Over, It Just Looks Different

"No I'm not. They just told me a few minutes ago that it's not happening today."

"Yes, you are. The doctor just told me you're going in today. They will be coming to get you soon."

Cindy arrived a few minutes later and I caught her up on the events of the day to that point. Still somewhat skeptical, we joked about the dinner tray that had been pulled away earlier in the week and how this might be another false alarm.

A little after 2 p.m., I was wheeled down to the waiting area outside of the operating rooms to wait, and the neurosurgeon came to review the options he'd laid out earlier in the week. Two minutes later, the anaesthetist and then a surgical nurse came to explain their roles and what they would be doing.

"I'm a little nervous," I told her.

"It says here you're legally blind," she said looking at my chart. "Is that right?"

"Yes I am. In fact, it was a complication from the last shunt revision that caused my sight loss."

"No wonder you're nervous!" she exclaimed.

I was wheeled into the brightly-lit operating room, which was buzzing with activity as a handful of staff prepared the room for my operation. The surgeon greeted me again and introduced me to the others in the room.

As the surgeon went back to his final preparations, I said to the nurse, "While you're in there, if you find the switch for my eyesight would you mind flipping it back on?"

The nurse laughed and called to the surgeon, "Did you hear that? He says while you're in there, if you find the switch for his eyesight he'd like you to turn it back on."

"You're going to feel a little bit warm in a minute," the anaesthetist said. "That's the medication that will put you to sleep." Almost immediately, I felt a warm sensation move up my body from my legs, through my chest and up to my head.

"Everybody, I'm starting to feel a little sleepy, so I'll see you all later," I said.

The next thing I remember was waking up in the recovery room — and I could still see! The surgeon came to see me a short time later. They had done a modified version of his plan A. They didn't change any of the shunt components as planned. Instead, he flushed out the blockage and left everything in place. I was just fine with that.

Life's Not Over, It Just Looks Different

The next day, Saturday, one of the residents came to check on me. I told him I felt really good, but we decided to wait another day before I went home. Being at the hospital is a lot easier to take when you know you're getting out the next day.

The clock can move a little slowly sometimes, but since it was Saturday night, I was able to catch two hockey games on television, and a friend came by for a visit, even though it was past visiting hours by then. The way I saw it, I was going home the next day, so the worst they could do was kick me out. I think the nurse knew that, too, and she allowed my visitor to stop by. We sat at the end of the hall chatting and laughing until nearly two in the morning.

The next morning (or perhaps I should say later that same morning) was Easter Sunday. I still felt great, so I put on my street clothes and waited to be released. This being another holiday, I wasn't sure when I would see a doctor, but since I had been seen about noon on Friday, I had a good feeling I wouldn't have to wait too long. Sure enough, by noon that day I was released from the hospital and had plenty of time to get home to change and freshen up before going to Easter dinner at Cindy's cousin's house.

STILL MOVING FORWARD

"Life is what happens to you while you're busy making other plans." —
John Lennon

I chose the title of this book, because I felt it captures how I feel about
everything that has happened since 2005. Life for Cindy and I looks
much different than I thought it would, both in our careers and in our
personal life, but it is certainly not over. If anything, I think I'm more
inspired to take on new challenges and to find ways to do the things I
enjoy.

I think the doctors knew all along that I would not fully recover my sight,
but didn't want to tell me that early on. I found out many years after the
surgery that when our family doctor filled out my paperwork for the
Disability Tax Credit, she listed my condition as permanent on the
forms, even though I was less than two months into my recovery at the
time. I believe the doctors wanted to give me time to come to my own
conclusions about my level of sight; along the way, I would figure out
how to use what I have.

I gave up my driver's licence for good when we moved to Alberta in
2012. At the registry office, I discovered they were going to make me
do an eye test before swapping my Ontario licence for one in our new
province. I could have taken the test and let the examiner revoke the
licence after the test results, but I chose to surrender it instead. In
Ontario, I wanted to keep my licence as a form of identification, but

Alberta has the Alberta ID card, so there was no need to keep my licence any longer.

Occasionally, I miss the convenience of driving, but most places I go around Calgary are transit accessible and, if not, Cindy does the driving. If I feel the urge to get behind the wheel of a vehicle, there is always the go-kart track. I went with a group of co-workers in the spring of 2015 for a night of racing at a local indoor track and, of the two races we ran, I took top spot in the first event and missed top spot in the second race by less than a quarter of a second.

Since driving is no longer an option, when I have the time and if the weather is pleasant, I actually prefer to walk many places. During our time in Toronto, I often went for walks lasting two or three hours at a time; when we moved to Calgary, the trend continued. I walk to or from work frequently, a distance of about 12 kilometres, and on my days off, I have two large park areas close to home to choose from.

Living my life in low resolution might have slowed me down somewhat, but there aren't many things it has completely stopped me from doing. For instance, reading a physical book is nearly impossible without the aid of my magnifier or CCTV unit, and even with those devices, reading paper pages is time-consuming and cumbersome. So, unless it's a book that I'm really eager to read or a textbook for a course that isn't available in any other format, I tend to avoid physical books. At first, I gravitated toward audio books, but I sometimes found the former broadcaster in me analysing the production value of the book, rather than listening to the content. As I once joked with a friend, you can take the boy out of broadcast, but you can't take broadcast out of the boy.

These days, with more and more books being made available electronically, I've taken to downloading books on my phone and having the voice over feature read the book to me. Initially, there was a bit of an adjustment getting used to the computerized voice, but now, it's my preferred way to read.

In 2013, I stopped working for a year and went back to school to study accounting and payroll administration, which I referred to as career choice 2A since it still involved numbers, but in a different way than what I was doing in the investment world. I really enjoyed learning something new and graduated with honours and a shiny new college diploma, but as I neared completion of the program, I realized the accounting world was a little too isolated for me. I found myself longing for a role where I could work with numbers, possibly do some teaching and, most importantly, work with people.

Roughly 15 months after finishing the college program, I brought those three things together when I started volunteering with Junior Achievement. Teaching junior high school students about investing through the Investment Strategies program was an amazing experience. Despite being in the school for only four days, I carried the positive energy from it with me for weeks afterward. Being involved with that program, I realized that it is truly what I want to do. Now, if only I could find a way to make a living at it. Was it possible to find a role that gave me that much happiness and get paid for it?

Since 2008, I had tried two different financial advisor roles, where I soon discovered selling mutual funds or credit cards were key elements of success and learned that those positions weren't a fit for me. Just when I was starting to think that my dream gig only existed in the volunteer world, I came across the role of a fee-for-service financial planner. As I write this section, I've enrolled in the first of the courses I'll need to achieve my goal of helping people with budgeting, saving and investing in a completely unbiased fashion, where the only thing I'll be selling is my time and knowledge. It's going to take some time, and I have plenty of studying ahead of me to make this dream a reality, but the end result will be worth the effort.

Like the quote at the beginning of this chapter suggests, life happens, and it can be greatly affected by changes to our physical and mental health, so I encourage everyone to find that balance between doing the things you have to do and the things you want to experience. We don't know when something will happen that could prevent us from achieving our goals or crossing items off of our to-do list. I believe everyone should set goals; the bigger the better; and go after them. If you achieve your goals or you're able to cross every item off your to-do list, great! Start a new list or set a new goal and go after it, too.

I use the term "to-do" because I'm far too young for a bucket list. Even as I reach my mid-forties, I'm still a kid at heart and I may never feel old enough for a bucket list, so instead, I have a "to-do" list. Being vision impaired has not stopped me from crossing a few items off my to-do list in the past ten years. I've skated on the Rideau Canal, gone down a zip-line and taken on the CN Tower Edge Walk in Toronto.

What happens from here? Who knows! The neurosurgeons have told me there will be more shunt revisions in my future. How many there are and when they happen are the unknowns that add a layer of mystery to my life. In the meantime, I'm still moving forward. My to-do list continues to grow; it changes from time to time and it contains both personal and professional things with one common theme — having fun. Because after all, I'm on this planet for fun.

The End

Life's Not Over, It Just Looks Different

AFTERWORD

Ten Reasons Losing My Sight Hasn't Been All Bad

10. Sleeping in until whenever I want. (So, why am I writing this at 7 a.m.?)

9. Free transit pass. (And pretty good transit service, too.)

8. Getting great customer service when I go shopping with the white cane.

7. Finding out that "Toronto the Good" is not just a slogan, it's actually out there.

6. Never missing a NASCAR race on television because I have to work. (Actually seeing the race on the screen is a different story.)

5. I still bowled over 200 when I went 5-pin bowling at Christmas.

4. Working with some great people from the CNIB.

3. Learning braille. (Although reading too much at once can cause "braille finger.")

2. Great support from my family, friends and especially my wife.

…and the number one reason losing my sight hasn't been all bad...

1.Never again hearing the question that haunts all men in relationships: "Honey do I look fat in this?"

ACKNOWLEDGEMENTS

Thank you to my mom, and my siblings Clayton and Chandra, for always being there when I need you. And in loving memory of my dad who is never far from my thoughts.

Thank you to my many aunts, uncles and cousins who have checked in for updates and been fantastic cheerleaders through the years. To our nephew Tristan, nieces Tianna, Nicole and Caitlin; because of you I have the greatest title in the world, "uncle".

Thank you to Marlene and Bob, whose hospitality, warmth and smiles have been greatly appreciated.

Thank you to Sofia for your positive energy and encouragement on this and other projects yet to be tackled.

Thank you to David Chilton for taking the time to call me and offer some advice on making this book happen.

A special thank you to Kim, Matt and Renée. We are blessed to have you in our lives. Your friendship during the good times has left lasting memories, and your support during the tough times will never be forgotten.

A special thank you also goes to Andrea. This book would not have gotten this far without you. Thank you for reading through the early

Life's Not Over, It Just Looks Different

versions and helping to shape what it has become. You're still the only one who can keep up with me on the long walks!

Thank you most of all to my wife Cindy, who has been my biggest cheerleader, fiercest protector and my best friend for more than 20 years. This book would not have happened without your love and support.

The closing credits:

Editing: Gayl Veinotte

Proofreading: Joanne Tomlins

Cover design: Cerridwen Hicks